THE DISCOVERY OF TEXAS

1528–1535

By Lawrence D. Sharp

How Cabeza de Vaca Survived and Where He Really Was

The Discovery of Texas 1528–1535
How Cabeza de Vaca Survived and Where He Really Was
By Lawrence D. Sharp

Cover art is by Eve Maulsby of Pearland, Texas

For permission requests, write to the publisher "Attention: Permissions Coordinator" at the address below:

lawrencesharp639@gmail.com

Table of Contents

*To my sons Brenan and Matthew
who, over the years of research, have
supported this project with enthusiasm.*

Preface

Álvar Núñez Cabeza de Vaca (1490?-1562?) thought he was doomed with the others in the expedition of Pánfilo de Narváez (d.1528) when his log barge sank in November 1528 off the Texas coast. After he stopped sobbing, he befriended the local Native Americans who eventually taught him to be a respected *físico* (physician). With his companions, he was the first non-native to explore Texas as he went from one village to another offering his healing services and prayers. The natives also taught him to barter with seashells and cane sticks so he could be a merchant. Later, his work as a *físico,* along with his optimistic faith, enabled him to make his way, with three others, to the corner of New Spain in northwestern Mexico. Passing from village to village he explored unknown lands, saw many people cured, made peace among enemies, and left a favorable legacy among the native people that lasted for decades.

The account of the survival of Cabeza de Vaca, who walked hundreds of miles through Texas and Mexico, is one of the earliest epics of the Americas. Only some 36 years before the 1527 start of the expedition, Christopher Columbus had discovered the New World in 1492. Only six years earlier, in 1521, Hernán Cortés had fought his way to victory over the Mexica-Aztec coalition, turning their city of Tenochtitlán into Mexico City. Because this journey took place so early in American history it is important that we

1

ascertain the specific geographic route he took, as well as the reasons for his survival.

I propose to tell the fascinating true story of how he discovered Texas and persevered through the long trek to New Spain. I also will show approximately where he was. Based on new methods of research and analysis, it is now possible to identify Malhado, the landmass onto which he crashed, as a shorter Galveston Island. We also can trace the entire route of his seven-year overland journey to Corazones, a village near the Pacific coast of Sonora, Mexico.

The lyrical narrative of Álvar Nuñez Cabeza de Vaca's journey as the first European to explore Texas should be well known. A few historians have tried to give him his due. In the late 1990s, as part of his television series on the conquest of the Americas, Michael Woods devoted an hour-long program to Cabeza de Vaca, along with such luminaries as Cortés and Pizarro, and his magnificent journey! On the other hand, in the United States, he has not always been widely recognized. Along with three others Cabeza de Vaca was the first outsider to explore and describe the natural features and the native people of Texas. Yet in this big state there are no counties or bridges or rivers named after him. There are no monuments erected in his honor.

Many of the Franciscan missionaries who made the long journey to San Antonio and built the Alamo and Mission San Jose were motivated by Cabeza de Vaca's little book, *Los Naufragios*, or The Shipwrecks. The missionaries who founded San Antonio did not realize that Cabeza de Vaca spent two summers (1533-34) in nearby Nopales, the place of many prickly pears. Moreover, it was Cabeza de Vaca who first suggested the San Antonio region, with its "lovely meadows," rivers, and other fine natural features, was a desirable place for a civilized people to build homes and ranches.

Having embarked on foot from the Texas coast on an extensive overland excursion through the interior, Cabeza de Vaca led three others in a brave attempt to stay alive. His quest to arrive at New Spain far to the south turned out to be a truly pioneering event.

Along with his companions, he was the first non-indigenous person, north of south-central Mexico, to travel from sea to sea or from the east side of the continent to the west. At the same time, he was the first outsider to explore the majestic landscape of what became the southwestern United States and northern Mexico.

Cabeza de Vaca was a rare example of a European *conquistador* who was humane in his dealings with the Native American people. In this, he was much like his contemporary Bartolomé de las Casas (1484-1566), who, although supportive of the conquest, wanted it done with methods and policies consistent with the Christian moral code, which included the virtues of mercy and love. Instead of employing the sword of violence, cruelty, and slavery, the Europeans should befriend the native people and, with peaceful and helpful methods, point them to a better way as Cabeza de Vaca exemplified on this very journey. If such values were followed, he argued, the native people would willingly turn to Christian ways and would cooperate with the conquerors. His thesis of conquest by friendship, teaching, and service will be more meaningful if we understand how he survived and where he was as he went from one native village to another through these vast lands of North America.

He and his three companions were indeed the first Europeans, and Esteban de Azamor, the first European of African descent, to explore the region that later became the United States, specifically Florida and Texas. If we count the three-to-four weeks of travel through Trans-Pecos, Texas, around October 1535, beginning with their landing on the Gulf Coast in late 1528, the explorers lived and worked in the Texas area of the United States for some six years and nine months. One could make the case that Cabeza de Vaca was the first non-native explorer, the first missionary, the first merchant, and the first physician to inhabit the lands of the United States. Moreover, long before others were brought to Virginia in 1619, Esteban de Azamor, a companion of Cabeza de Vaca, was the first African slave here in the United States.

These four Spaniards, three white and one black, were the first outsiders not only to inhabit but also to penetrate the interior of the United States. An explanation of how they did it and the identification of the geographic sites of their travel are crucial to a full understanding of what they accomplished. In the late 1400s and early 1500s, European *conquistadores* had entered the Caribbean islands, Central America, South America, and south-central Mexico. By 1528, their ships already had passed along the Gulf and Atlantic coasts of the United States; but no European prior to the journey of Cabeza de Vaca had traveled more than a few miles beyond the shore of the States.

In 1521, Juan Ponce de León (1460-1521) attempted to make a settlement in the area that became Florida, and in 1526, Lucas Vázquez de Ayllón (1475-1526) attempted to do the same in the area that became South Carolina. However, neither went more than a few miles inland nor stayed more than a few months. Prior to any of the other notable expeditions, Cabeza de Vaca and three companions walked far into the areas that became the United States and northern Mexico.

Reports of a wealthy city "to the north," as stated by Cabeza de Vaca and the others at the successful conclusion of this long trip, became the cause of the early journeys of Marcos de Niza (1539) and Francisco Vázquez de Coronado (1540-42) into Arizona and New Mexico. Herein, I will explain how Cabeza de Vaca inadvertently sent Coronado into the "far away" lands to the north in search of a wealthy civilization that was not there. To appreciate this series of early expeditions, we must know the approximate location of the village of Corazones as well as by what route the four men came upon it.

The description of the voyage and of the native people in his report, *Los Naufragios,* to the king became the motivation for two notable Franciscan missionary journeys, that of Agustín Rodríguez (1581-82) and the one led by Antonio de Espejo (1582-83). These expeditions were foundational stepping-stones that, by 1598, led to

4

a permanent European settlement in New Mexico. Along with those on the coast of Florida, these were the earliest European settlements in the lands of the United States. If we examine the precise route taken by Cabeza de Vaca, it will illuminate all the missionary, exploratory, and migratory work that he stimulated.

How can we ascertain the route of Cabeza de Vaca from Galveston on the coast of Texas to Corazones on the lower reaches of the Río Yaqui just north of Ciudad Obregon in Sonora, Mexico? I have set forth a simple hypothesis: the path can be traced accurately by following the fresh water of rivers and creeks. Under the guidance of the Amerindian people, Cabeza de Vaca traversed established footpaths near sources of drinking water in the age before horses were available. The trails simply tracked the course of a river, not necessarily on the riparian bank, but roughly parallel to it and within reasonable walking distance to get a drink. Some travel segments were overland spans of a typical one-day walk of some 20 miles or less between creeks. Still others ascended upstream to the head or source of one creek or river on an elevated divide such as a mountain or a hill and then crossed over to pick up a second stream or river near its head so as to follow it downstream.

In the two original narratives of the expedition, there are, in fact, inadvertent references to rivers and creeks scattered throughout. Cabeza de Vaca and his three companions undoubtedly thought they were merely following trails through the country without realizing that they were never far from fresh water. They were always near flowing streams except for those times when they were on the island of Malhado (Galveston) and the peninsula of Aransas (Blackjack Peninsula). Moreover, the reality on the ground, ascertained by means of Google Earth, good traditional maps, digital or computer maps, some personal visits within Texas, and other topographical aides provide a route that is consistent with the principal of proximity to fresh water and which, at the same time, is congruent with the written evidence.

5

This is a complete revision of my Kindle ebook published in 2015, under the title <u>The True Path of the First European Explorer of Texas: Chronicling the Amazing Journey of Cabeza de Vaca</u>. Please send reviews and comments to me at <u>lawrencesharp639@gmail.com</u>.

Chapter 1
The Landing on Galveston Island

On a chilly November afternoon in 1528, Álvar Núñez Cabeza de Vaca (1490?-1562?), a gentler kind of Spanish *conquistador,* faced 100 Native Americans, each with a long bow and a quiver of arrows, and who stood at a distance staring at him and his thirty-nine grisly companions.[1] Since one of his compatriots had taken some fish, a clay pot, and a dog from their empty village, Cabeza de Vaca knew the local men had reason to be angry. With the sea to his back, he pondered what to do about these tall, sturdy men who had segments of cane stuck in their pierced lips. "In our fear, they appeared to be giants," he later wrote.[2]

After their log raft crashed onto this remote barrier island a few hours earlier, Cabeza de Vaca and his weary men wrapped themselves tightly in their shirts and coats and gathered around several hot bonfires. A cold wind blew in from the murky, brownish-blue ocean. The Spaniards were too weak to push their boat into the water and continue their journey by sea along the Texas coast. Badly in need of some food and fresh water, they had floated, starving and thirsty, for more than a week, helplessly lost in the Gulf of Mexico. Having already, on several occasions, defended themselves against native attacks in Florida, and at an earlier stop along the way, they waited for a signal to lift their swords for yet another fight.

Confronted by the row of armed men and later by other enormous obstacles, Cabeza de Vaca found a way around, as we shall see, and eventually made the long trip home. For centuries, two questions have emerged from the two primary accounts of the overland journey that began on the sandy beach of that green, wooded island. How is it that he, with three others, walked barefoot from the coast of the Gulf of Mexico to the coast of the Gulf of California? Secondly, what route did they take from this landmass on which they went ashore? With a new method of analysis, the manner in which he traveled safely will be revealed, and for the first time, the route of the overland journey will be correctly delineated, all in refutation of the proposals of Harbert Davenport (1882-1957), which have served as the conventional wisdom on the subject for over a century.[3]

From that Texas beach, Cabeza de Vaca, the Spanish king's financial agent of this failed expedition, meandered on the earliest journey by a non-native across Texas. He walked through the deep green forests that lined the Brazos River near the suburbs of Houston and followed the Texas Colorado River to just east of Austin. He gathered prickly pears in the "lovely meadows" and hills in the region just south of the city of San Antonio. With three other survivors, Esteban de Azamor (1500?-1539), Andrés Dorantes de Carranza (1500?-1555?), and Alonso del Castillo Maldonado (1510?-1565?), he hiked through Big Bend National Park, the Davis Mountains, and across northern Mexico to the Pacific coast. Along the way he discovered the Rio Grande. He was the first to see and describe thousands of bison on the Great Plains. After he finally arrived in Mexico City, he inadvertently sent Coronado on his expedition of 1540-42 into Arizona and New Mexico to find a wealthy city that was not there.

On top of these stellar accomplishments, Cabeza de Vaca helped to open the door to the eventual settlement of the lands of the United States by publishing *Los Naufragios,* The Shipwrecks, the account of his long journey through the wilderness. He also motivated Franciscan missionaries to go north to the regions along and beyond the Rio Grande. In 1598 the missionaries helped to establish an early colony in New Mexico and, in 1718, the mission that became the city of San Antonio.[4]

His book and a second narrative, *Historia General,* by Gonzalo Fernando de Oviedo y Valdez, provide bits and pieces of information about the island on which they landed and the other sites through which they passed, although the interpreter struggles with difficulties in both volumes. Oviedo frequently makes faulty attempts to summarize and arrange his main source, now lost, called the *Joint Report,* a sort of deposition of three of the survivors. Cabeza de Vaca leaves us with various gaps, conundrums, and errors.[5] Nonetheless, these evidentiary problems can be resolved, allowing us to ascertain the path the explorers traversed and how they did it.

Slender and of medium height, the *conquistador* who faced 100 armed men on the shores of Texas was a clever, winsome fellow with a sly sense of humor. While he was highly moral and sincerely devout, he also aspired to find silver, gold, and glory in the New World and win acclaim from the Spanish king who had appointed him royal treasurer of this disaster-prone expedition. In the belief that he was born into a line of high achievers, he wanted to bring honor to his mother's family name of Cabeza de Vaca (head of cow).[6] "I thought that my deeds and services would be as illustrious ... as those of my ancestors," he later reflected, and that I would offer a "greater service" than merely to write the account *Los Naufragios.*[7] It seems he was unaware that by surviving and making a record of it, he would be remembered honorably by many more people than any of his forebears.

Prior to landing on the island where he stood facing the armed men, Cabeza de Vaca had persevered through multiple crises that plagued the project from the first. After arriving from Spain in late July 1527, during their brief stay at Santo Domingo in the Dominican Republic, scores of recruits deserted. Cabeza de Vaca however stayed loyal to the expedition and to its goal to find great wealth and establish a colony in the unknown lands north of the "Río de Las Palmas," which was the Río Soto La Marina in Tamaulipus. When over a hundred more men and two ships were lost in a hurricane as the fleet tarried on the southern coast of Cuba, Cabeza de Vaca gave thanks that he was spared and continued his duties.

The fleet of ships finally embarked, but the confused pilot missed the target destination by hundreds of miles, and the explorers went ashore in May of 1528, on the wrong side of the Gulf of Mexico.[8] Cabeza de Vaca protested in vain when the head of the expedition, Governor Pánfilo de Narváez (1490-1528), ineptly sent the ships on ahead to wait for Cabeza de Vaca and his men at the mouth of the Las Palmas. Narváez wanted, in the interim, to find and conquer "Apalachee," which was reported to be a large city full of gold and other riches. Since they had not arrived in the region of the Las Palmas in Tamaulipas but near Tampa Bay in Florida, they never met the ships. Cabeza de Vaca, Narváez, Dorantes, and the rest of the 300 members of the expedition slowly made their way north up the peninsula, where they found Apalachee to be a modest village of 40 humble grass huts with no gold or other wealth.[9]

In September 1528, after losing some 50 men, most of whom were killed by Native Americans, Cabeza de Vaca and the others built and boarded five large, rickety log rafts, three of which sank or fell to ruin within six weeks at sea. Both Cabeza de Vaca and Andrés Dorantes were co-captains of one of the vessels. Cabeza de Vaca navigated his flat, log boat down a river, likely the Ochlockonee south of Tallahassee. Just offshore, in tandem, the five barges, each with forty-eight to fifty famished soldiers, followed the coastline westbound in search of a small Spanish village near the mouth of the Río Pánuco which was then at the northeast frontier of New Spain.[10]

By the time the weary travelers reached the coast of Mississippi, they had no fresh water and only a little food. Twice they attempted to go ashore for water and food, but hostile bands forced them to embark again. The starving men were then driven by the powerful flow of the Mississippi River out to sea where, over eight to ten days, they were at the mercy of storms and currents that eventually swept them toward Texas. At one point, Cabeza de Vaca begged the governor to try to keep the boats together, but Narváez refused. He later went ashore south of San Antonio Bay where local people attacked and killed most of the men on his and one of the other barges.

Meanwhile, Cabeza de Vaca, Andrés Dorantes, and the men on each of their two rafts were desperately trying to get to land so they could find some fresh water to drink. There was neither time nor desire to navigate around to a better landing site in a lagoon on the inland side of an island or peninsula. About five miles apart, both vessels finally crashed onto the seaward beach of what the Spaniards named the *Isla de Malhado*, the Island of Misfortune, where Cabeza de Vaca was pondering what to do about the native men who were staring at him and the others.

The name the Spaniards gave it belies the notably good features of the island of bad luck. While the local indigenous people were, on other barrier islands farther down the shore, killing their expedition compatriots, the two bands, the "Han" and the "Capoques," who lived on Malhado part of the year, were friendly and generous to the European strangers.[11] Crucially, the island had plenty of fresh water and food, including edible roots and fish. Also, there were lots of trees with fallen branches for the campfires, all factors that coincide with prehistoric Galveston Island, but not Folletts San Luis Peninsula.

Most historians following Davenport have pointed to Folletts San Luis Peninsula, also known as Velasco or Oyster Bay, as the true Malhado; however, it isn't large enough; it does not have fresh water at both ends and is practically treeless.[12] If the league measurement of Cabeza de Vaca was three miles as the evidence suggests, Malhado could have been a segment of Galveston Island; whereas, Folletts is not an island but a peninsula. No archaeological evidence of Native American habitation has been unearthed on Folletts as it has been on Galveston.[13] Before San Luis Island grew into its northeast end in 1935, the northeast peninsula part of Folletts San Luis stretched out to only about seven miles, not fifteen as required by the record.[14] Folletts is too narrow as well, only a half mile or less over most of its length; Galveston Island, with an average width of one and one-half miles, matches what was stated by Cabeza de Vaca.[15] Furthermore, as we will see, the description of the movement of the Dorantes group down the shoreline in April 1529 reveals that Malhado could not have been Folletts San Luis Peninsula and had to have been a shorter Galveston Island.[16]

On the beach of Malhado on that eventful November day, Cabeza de Vaca decided to attempt to make peace with the armed men. Governor Narváez never would have done something like this. Not inclined to be friendly to the Native Americans, he instead left a trail of cruelty, violence, and hostility in Cuba and in Florida. The respectful act of Cabeza de Vaca illustrates how, by making friends and learning from the native inhabitants, he became the first European to explore deeply into the interior of the United States in Florida and Texas - and survive.

His approach was risky yet simple. The Spaniards had brought along some cheap trinkets to use in barter. With another man, Cabeza de Vaca walked up and, using signs and gestures, tried "the best that they could ... to assure them" they meant no harm. He offered some little beads and bells. The local men could have reacted with fear or hostility against the strangers. Instead they responded by giving Cabeza de Vaca arrows, and later they brought food and water.[17]

After a few days, when Cabeza de Vaca and his men recovered enough strength to resume the journey southwest down the coast, they stripped to dig their flat log boat out of the sand. It was a difficult task that apparently took several hours. Finally, they threw their belongings onto it and pushed away from shore. With good luck followed by bad, a big wave broke the raft apart, and it sank; three men drowned. Since his friend Lope de Oviedo could not swim, it appears that Cabeza de Vaca had to pull him back to shore where he and the others fell exhausted onto the sandy beach.[18] Now wet and freezing with nothing to cover themselves, no shirts, no pants, no shoes, they quickly gathered more tree branches and built new bonfires using embers from those of the night before.

A short while before sundown, as he huddled in the sand dunes naked and cold, with the open sea on one side and an unknown continent on the other, Cabeza de Vaca began to realize how hopeless things were. When he and his companions arrived at Malhado, they were, though frail and weary, still elegantly dressed, armed *conquistadores* of the Spanish empire who looked with pity on the poor, almost-naked indigenous people. Now, it was the Europeans who were naked, poor, and vulnerable. The local bands had food, water, shelter, and the knowledge to survive. The roles had been reversed.

As long as they had a seaworthy vessel, they could continue down the shore to *Nueva España,* New Spain, but now it was gone. A rescue was out of the question. No one in Havana or Santo Domingo, the two major centers of the Caribbean, knew where they were. All of their possessions, their clothing, swords— everything had been lost in the sea along with the raft itself, which was their only means, or so it seemed at the time, of traveling to Pánuco or some other part of the small political entity in south-central Mexico. To reach any part of New Spain, they would have to cross a wide lagoon to the mainland and make a long, arduous voyage on foot through unknown lands inhabited by strange people, some of whom may be hostile. Faced with a task that appeared to be impossible, Cabeza de Vaca was driven to his knees, figuratively if not literally. The others joined him as he wept, desperately begging for pardon for his sins and a way to go home.[19]

After a while, Cabeza de Vaca noticed through his tears that a group of the local men had drawn near but started to leave. Having come with more food and water, they were startled to see these bearded strangers, now without their clothes, wailing and distraught. Disregarding his men, who thought they would be killed if they went to the village, he jumped up to chase them down, and later he asked to be taken "to their houses."[20] While his fellow *conquistadores* did not receive the same vision, Cabeza de Vaca was given on that forsaken beach the mercy of an optimistic confidence that, with the aid of the native people, he could find his way back.

After Cabeza de Vaca explained through signs what had happened, the native people looked with compassion on the Europeans and wept with them for half an hour. When they understood his request, the natives took the naked *conquistadores* to their village, having built bonfires along the path to keep them warm. The next day Cabeza de Vaca learned another expedition barge also had come ashore on Malhado a few miles away. Undressed, Cabeza de Vaca soon met a fully clothed Captain Andrés Dorantes, his friend with whom he had worked on projects in Florida earlier that year (1528), coming down with his men from the other end of the island. It must have lifted his spirit when Dorantes told Cabeza de Vaca that the second barge, though damaged, could be fixed. If Dorantes arrived in New Spain, he could send a ship back to get them.

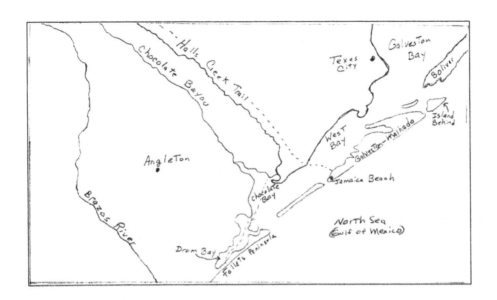

Map 1 -THE FORM OF PREHISTORIC GALVESTON ISLAND. The Isla de Malhado must have been, in 1528, a heavily wooded, shorter Galveston Island about 15.0 miles long. The two ends were at the southernmost part of the town of Jamaica Beach and near the southern part of Ferry Road with a small "island behind" off the northeast point.

Chapter 2
Dorantes Leaves Cabeza de Vaca Behind

W e agreed to fix up" the log barge of Dorantes, Cabeza de Vaca recorded.[21] No doubt the local people watched with curiosity as he and the other Europeans inspected the vessel on the shore of Malhado. On the northeast seashore of Galveston Island where now there is a seawall and a line of tourist hotels, in 1528 there would have been parallel to the shore a row of grass and weeds. Trees and brush grew to the west of this green line and the log boat was settled in a wide strip, fifty yards or more at low tide, of white-to-gray beach silt and sand that sloped down from the greenery to the ocean.

All the desires of the Spaniards to save their lives and to escape from this remote spot were centered on that crude raft. If they could send it, loaded with the healthiest half of the men from two groups, to Pánuco at the border of New Spain, a rescue of the others could be arranged. They set to work making repairs and preparations, but some of the horsehair straps were, it appears, already rotten and could no longer hold together the big logs. When pushed into the water for a test, this one also fell apart and sank, and with it, all hope for an exit from Malhado by sea.

A day or two before this, when he got up from his prayers and sobs in the dunes after his own log barge broke up, Cabeza de Vaca was possessed by a vision that he would indeed arrive in New Spain. From there, the place he called a "land of Christians," he would go home to Europe. Nonetheless, with the loss of the second barge, he once again faced the reality of an uncertain journey to the southwest. Neither he nor the others knew that Pánuco near Tampico was a long distance, over 550 miles down the seashore, and the way was blocked by large bays and by certain violent indigenous bands who oppressed their guests.

Except for the herculean task of finding enough food and fresh water, the greatest threat was to be assaulted by a hostile native or a wild animal. While Dorantes and those who had been on his log barge still had theirs, Cabeza de Vaca and his companions had, when their vessel broke up, lost their swords along with everything else; he would be helpless if attacked. He could survive and make the long journey only if he found a way to travel peacefully among the indigenous people. We know that eventually he arrived at the Yaqui delta in northwest Mexico, but by what route? How did he, with a few others, cross the unknown lands that became Texas and northern Mexico? Other than Galveston Island, which parts of Texas did he visit?

About this time, later in November 1528, five "great swimmers" led by Figueroa de Toledo, volunteered, despite the uncertainties and the cold weather, to try to work their way down the coast to New Spain. Dorantes was eager to go but not until there was warmer weather. While Cabeza de Vaca was a good swimmer, he refused to leave any of his men behind, some of whom were too frail to travel or could not swim. The weak and the sick must not be deserted, he later explained, and "whatever might happen to one would happen to all without anyone abandoning another."[22] Cabeza de Vaca drafted these words as a cryptic censure of Dorantes who abandoned him not once during the odyssey, but twice.

Waiting for spring when they could follow Figueroa along the shore to the southwest, the 75 or so men of the two groups, lived through December, January, and February on opposite ends of the *Isla de Malhado*. The reference to "both parts," *ambas partes,* may indicate a natural boundary on the island between the respective territories, such as the inlet called Sweetwater Lake that nearly cuts Galveston Island in two. In the part referred to as *atrás,* or back, to the northeast where his raft made landfall, Dorantes and his men lived as guests of the Han, whom Cabeza de Vaca referred to as "the others." In the part described as *adelante,* or ahead, to the southwest, the royal treasurer and his group stayed with the Capoques.[23] During this time, the Europeans were digging roots, gathering firewood, and burying their companions one by one as they died of a stomach illness. This unknown disease decimated the people of both villages so that by April, only half of them were left alive. Eventually, Cabeza de Vaca himself fell ill and thought it was the end of his life.

By walking, swimming, and riding in a log canoe, Figueroa and the other four swimmers made their way to Arboleda, the region of forests on the lower Guadalupe River. Here they were stopped in their march to New Spain, as were Dorantes and Cabeza de Vaca later in the saga.[24] They were all prevented from traveling farther down the shore of Texas, not only by more lagoons but also by the local Native Americans. Unlike the hospitable people of the two communities on Malhado, they made the foreigners captives, commanded them to do servile chores, hit them with sticks, tormented them with threats, and would not permit them to go to the regions further inland.

Figueroa and the other "great swimmers" had to submit to this form of coerced labor, and their new masters did not give them much food at first. Most of the pecans in the area apparently had been gathered before the swimmers arrived in early to mid-December 1528. The winter weather was severe, and they found little to eat. Except for Figueroa, all the swimmers died or were killed within a few weeks.[25]

One day in the forests of Arboleda, a native man led an astonished Figueroa to another European! After the two men recovered from the shock of finding each other in the wilderness, Hernando de Esquivel, who was desperately trying to survive a perilous situation, told Figueroa that almost all the men on two of the barges had been slaughtered or had died of starvation or illness soon after they came ashore.[26] The head of the expedition, Governor Narváez, was last seen just off the coast, likely of San Jose Island, ill and weak, with two other men on his raft.

Esquivel told Figueroa that, since Narváez and the vessel were gone the next morning, they presumed he had been driven by the winds and the currents out to sea where he, too, expired. Cabeza de Vaca and Dorantes later learned that local native people also killed all those on the fifth barge that landed still farther down the coast on San Jose or Mustang Island.[27] Figueroa begged Esquivel to join him in an attempt to escape and continue the journey to Pánuco and New Spain. Esquivel declined.

Back in the region of Malhado in early March 1529, Dorantes, along with Castillo, the son of a Spanish physician, Esteban, an African slave sometimes called "Steven the Black" or "Estebanico;" and ten or twelve more survived the stomach epidemic. These men crossed in Han canoes to the mainland where they spent a month with their hosts feeding on oysters, fish, and blackberries.[28] The six-mile, two league, canoe trip to the mainland from the northeast Han part of the island coincides with a route between the sites of downtown Galveston and Texas City, a fact that Davenport ignored. The latter town sits on a kind of mound about ten feet above sea level. Nearby Moses Bayou or another creek may have provided the Han with water and with firewood from trees along the banks.[29] The water would have been partly brackish, but they drank it anyway.

The record implies there were two primary canoe routes to the mainland from Malhado, one at each end of the island. Because we are told that a six-mile northeast pass of the Han was the widest, we conclude the Capoque canoe route across from the southwest end was probably less than four miles.[30] These spans are consistent with a shorter Galveston Island as the real Malhado but not with Folletts

San Luis Peninsula as Davenport posited. The latter land mass would have been too close to the mainland.[31]

Not wanting to stay another day on the forsaken island of bad luck, restless Dorantes gathered his group in early April to make an attempt to reach the little Spanish post he had heard about that was located near the mouth of the Río Pánuco. They made the half-day trip down to the southwest portion of Malhado to recruit Cabeza de Vaca and his barge companions whom they had not seen for up to four months. Unaware of intervening bays and rivers, he and his men, now numbering thirteen or fourteen, planned to walk *adelante*, or forward, and generally to the west, along the seashore with the water of the ocean at their feet on the left.

While Andrés Dorantes and Cabeza de Vaca were friends who both received appointment from Charles V (1500-1558), the Emperor of the Holy Roman Empire and King of Spain, they were quite different in both temperament and character. Dorantes had no moral qualms that interfered with his survival instinct, whereas the royal treasurer was tempered by deep convictions. Dorantes summarily abandoned the only two European men still alive on the Capoque end of Malhado. One of these was Lope de Oviedo who was too ill to travel. Dorantes apparently thought nothing of leaving behind Lope to suffer alone in the wilderness while Cabeza de Vaca waited for him for three years.

Informed that Cabeza de Vaca was tarrying on the mainland with his host family, Dorantes and his group passed in canoes over the adjacent bay, from the southwest part of Malhado to the mainland opposite; however, it was not a free ride. Earlier, the Han ferried them to and from the northeast part of the island with no mention of a fare because they were their guests. However, the Dorantes group had no special relationship with the Capoques, and to cross they had to pay a hefty price.

Dorantes still had a sword, shoes, shirt, and pants; although, all of it would soon be stolen by some of the cruel people of Arboleda. He also possessed a valuable fur coat obtained earlier from a village chief and which could have been used as a blanket on cold nights. He would not have offered the fur coat as payment if the bay could be forded easily. The fact that he surrendered the coat as fare indicates the lagoon on the route taken was of sufficient depth and breadth to require a vessel.

If the inlets were similar in dimension to what they have been in the historical period, West Bay, adjacent to Galveston Island, was sufficiently deep and wide to justify a canoe. However, the men easily could have waded across Drum Bay, only one-to-two feet deep at low tide, and the other shallow, narrow lagoons next to Folletts-San Luis Peninsula.[32] On the other hand, to cross from Galveston Island to Carancahua Point on the mainland opposite Jamaica Beach, canoes were needed. The bay at that longitude is three to three-and-a-half miles wide and, in places, five to six feet deep at low tide.

When they got out of the canoes after crossing from Malhado to the mainland, Dorantes and his group began to look for Cabeza de Vaca, who had fallen seriously ill at a Capoque camp farther inland.[33] If from the area of Carancahua Point they followed an established foot path alongside a stream to a Capoque village near some trees, the road ran upstream to the only one there - Halls Creek, or Halls Bayou. Looking for an interior route to New Spain, it is likely that Cabeza de Vaca later followed this same Halls Creek Trail that took him west by northwest to the village of the Charuccos. He suggests this community was in *los montes*, the woods, which is probably a designation of the forest along the bend in the Brazos River. On the way upstream, Dorantes and his group were met by one or more Capoques. By signs or gestures not fully understood, the Capoques may have attempted to communicate that an illness had left Cabeza de Vaca prostrate. Impatient Dorantes did not bother to check; instead, he assumed his compatriot was dead and turned his group forthwith to abandon the search.[34]

Desiring to walk down the beach to the southwest, the Dorantes group now went to a different lagoon, *otro ancón*, over which they were ferried in exchange for certain things, *ciertas cosas*, perhaps some glass beads. There can be little doubt that this different lagoon was Chocolate Bay combined with the connected inlets of Bastrop, Christmas, and Drum.[35] After they crossed the second bay in canoes, they walked about six miles to what is described as "a large river which was beginning to grow [rise] because of the floods and rains."[36]

On the Four Rivers Trail, they walked down the beach or "along the coast" approximately nine miles, (three leagues), to a second river, the San Bernard. Then they went to another one, Caney Creek, farther along by nine to twelve miles, (three or four leagues). Finally, they traveled fifteen to eighteen miles to a fourth river, the Texas Colorado River, (five to six leagues farther), all estimated years later.

If Dorantes and his men took some inland route across the four rivers as most books say, they could not have watched helplessly as several compatriots drowned. Their little, improvised rafts were driven out to sea. Nor could they have described a peninsula, or "point," located just past the fourth river mouth, whose white sand dunes were visible from "far out" to sea.[37] From the mouth of the Mississippi River to the mouth of the Rio Grande, there is no span of less than fifty miles with four river mouths opening to the sea- except at one segment of shoreline – that between the former mouth of the Brazos River and the Texas Colorado River.

Because the first flooded river that Dorantes encountered after disembarking from the canoes was "large" and was about nine miles from the second, it had to have been the Brazos. Although Davenport named it the first river, little Oyster Creek is quite shallow and drains to a small basin; it does not match the description of this "large river."[38] Moreover, if Oyster Creek were the first, then the second would have been the Brazos, and the appropriate walking distance would be two to four miles, which diverges sharply from the nine miles, three leagues, in the narrative.[39]

The former mouth of the Brazos River is the deciding landmark to confirm the identity of Malhado which, as is the case with Galveston Island, had to have been located *atrás*, back, or to its northeast. From the 1500s and until 1929, the natural Brazos mouth, which must not be confused with the artificial one several miles down the shore, was located between the little seaside towns of Quintana and Surfside Beach, (formerly Velasco).

Corresponding to Malhado as a shorter Galveston Island, Dorantes rode a canoe from its southwest part to the mainland over a lagoon, West Bay, of such width and depth to require a vessel. He then turned back to cross a different lagoon, Chocolate Bay, so as to arrive near the seashore about six miles northeast of the former mouth of the Brazos.[40] To go to the mainland opposite Folletts San Luis Peninsula, canoes would not have been necessary, and there would have been no need to pay the high price of a fur coat for a ride. The group could have waded through shallow Drum Bay, or if Folletts San Luis were a peninsula, they could have walked around its southwest end.[41] From the mainland opposite the southwest part of Folletts San Luis Peninsula, there would have been no second bay to cross to go to the former Brazos mouth![42]

Losing two who drowned in the attempt, a little more than ten miles farther down, rounded off in the record to nine miles, or three leagues, the Dorantes party crossed the flooded mouth of the second river, the San Bernard. They pressed ahead another "three or four leagues" to Caney Creek, which flows through the town of Sargent and poured directly into the sea at the same place in the early 1500s as it did in the 1800s. Eventually, it was diverted, as were all the coastal rivers and creeks, to make way for the Gulf Intracoastal Waterway.[43] Fitting nicely with the narrative evidence, this third river mouth, where the Europeans found one of the five barges ruined and abandoned, was about thirteen miles from the San Bernard.[44]

The span from the former mouth of Caney Creek to that of the Texas Colorado is about twenty-four miles. Although the distance is farther than the fifteen-to-eighteen miles of the rough estimate in the narrative, it is close enough to name the Colorado the fourth river whose waters emptied directly into the Gulf of Mexico prior to its diversion into Matagorda Bay. In an earlier age, the Texas Colorado mouth was identical to that of Caney Creek, but the two bodies of water have been separated since about the year AD 1000.[45]

After some of the local Deaguanes people gave them a canoe ride over the Colorado, the Dorantes group soon arrived at a "large" and "deep" bay that was almost three miles, one league, in width behind a "point," or peninsula with white sand dunes that extended out to sea, all congruent with the eastern wing of Matagorda Bay.[46] The same local Deaguanes people furnished one or more canoes by which the Dorantes group, including Castillo and Esteban, passed over a large lagoon, Matagorda Bay, and a smaller one beyond it, San Antonio Bay.[47] This canoe trip from the easternmost part of Matagorda Bay to the entrance of San Antonio Bay, perhaps broken by an overnight stay at the mid-point of Port O'Connor, was about thirty-six miles, or twelve leagues, one narrative says. The distance to the head of San Antonio Bay was about forty-five miles as the other narrative indicates.[48]

After Dorantes left him behind, Cabeza de Vaca recovered from his illness and continued, until the spring of 1530, to live with the Capoques on the island and on the nearby mainland opposite. If, as is likely, the island village of the Capoques was in the area of the Mitchell Ridge archaeological site on Galveston Island, near Lafitte's Cove on the southwest bank of Eckert Bayou, then he and his group may have crashed ashore some two miles to the east near the site of the Sand Dollar Beach House on Buena Vista Drive. The Dorantes barge made landfall four or five miles to the northeast of this point, perhaps somewhere near the end of what is now 89th

Street, in Han territory just beyond the inlet called Sweetwater Lake.[49]

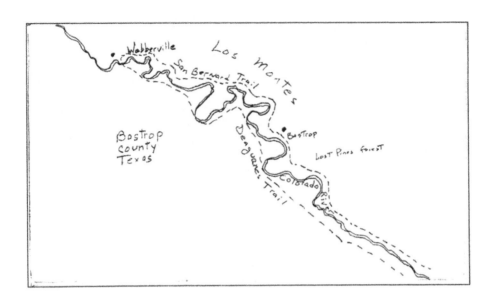

Map 2- THE FORESTS OF LOS MONTES. Going west by northwest alongside the Texas Colorado River, the royal treasurer walked through the site of Bastrop and likely as far as Webberville before turning back on the Deaguanes Trail to return to the sea.

Chapter 3
Cabeza de Vaca Becomes a Físico

While Dorantes, Castillo, Esteban, and a few others were trying to survive as slaves in the lands that encompassed the lower Guadalupe River and Aransas on Blackjack Peninsula, the royal treasurer of the expedition "was seeking out by what way I was to go later on."[50] He was making plans for the long journey to Veracruz, Mexico City, or some part of the new nation far to the south. From there he wanted to go back to his home in Spain and to María, his Jewish *converso* wife, and make a report to his king. Toward this end, he quickly sensed the importance of communicating with the local indigenous people. In only a few months after the landing on Malhado, he was sufficiently conversant in the local Capoque dialect to have an exchange of ideas with his host, Principal, about illness, healing, and remedies.[51]

They may have been sitting near a campfire while eating roots or fish when Principal surprised Cabeza de Vaca with a proposition—that he learn the practices and rituals of a *físico,* or physician.[52] It was a mandate to labor, as did the native *curadores* or healers, with the sick and injured one at a time with rites of rubbing, sucking, and blowing, among other techniques. The *físicos* employed hot rocks and living things found "in the country," the record says, which may be a reference to certain herbs, roots, bark, and leaves.[53] One of the French survivors of the LaSalle expedition to this section of coastal Texas in the 1680s observed how the native *físicos* practiced the same "sucking of wounds" and such, and, based on their "marvelous knowledge of the different properties of the medicinal herbs that abound in the whole country" with "much success" they could "easily heal themselves."[54]

Cabeza de Vaca was unaware that Principal, the man with whom he lived, was the Capoque chief and did not at first realize how serious he was. Quite apart from what he thought of the native remedies, he probably had flashes in his mind of the many hours of individual attention to patients such a responsibility would entail. He rejected the invitation to take the office and even ventured a joke about the efforts of the indigenous physicians to heal their suffering patients. Principal took the remark as an insult. In an act that revealed his authority as lord of the community, he angrily grabbed the roots or fish that Cabeza de Vaca was eating and threatened to withhold all food until he agreed.

The exchange that is summarized in *Los Naufragios* reflects previous conversations between the two men, such as one would expect between a guest and host. From time to time, as a kind of lay missionary teacher, Cabeza de Vaca tried to tell the native people about the good creator God who should be worshipped, and his moral commandments obeyed. It appears that Principal had respectfully listened to his guest, but now he was quite indignant with him and responded with something like this amplified paraphrase:

"You have greater knowledge and virtue than we, but in this matter, you are wrong. I know from experience that stones from the ground and herbs from the country have power to heal. I have seen that by placing a hot stone on the abdomen, the pain there is removed and the sick person restored to health."[55]

At some point during that first year and a half in Texas, in which he assumed the duties of a healer, Cabeza de Vaca also was put on notice that he could safely travel to other villages if he went as an unarmed trader. Principal and the other Capoques may have encouraged him to travel inland with cane sticks, seashells, and other items found on the coast so he could return later with things they themselves wanted that were more readily available farther inland. Some flint arrowheads were found in 1962-63 at a prehistoric habitation site at the southern corner of the town of Jamaica Beach on the southwest Capoque end of Galveston Island.[56] Since the nearest sites to obtain flint stones to make arrowheads and knives were more than fifty miles away, it is likely that they were dependent on traveling merchants.

With his introduction to the vocations of trader and healer, the barefoot *conquistador* now possessed the tools and status whereby he could traverse the continent. At about this point, he began to barter when he could, and he offered his healing services everywhere he went among the indigenous people. In the early years, until the fall of 1532 when he arrived in Arboleda on the lower Guadalupe River, his work as a *físico* and his reputation as a merchant won him a friendly welcome from village to village. However, as we shall see, it was not until the summer of 1535, when he walked into Cincuenta, the community of fifty houses in far south Texas, that his standing as a healer lifted him and three others to lofty social heights of celebrity and began to propel them safely across the continent to New Spain.

Probably in October 1529, so we may calculate, Cabeza de Vaca was trained in the healing arts. He was living in a Capoque village that was likely near the Mitchell Ridge archaeological dig on the southwest bank of Eckert Bayou in the area of Lafitte's Cove.[57] Years later, in 1532, after he arrived in Arboleda on the lower Guadalupe River and began treating patients there, his companion, Castillo, decided he too would become a *físico*. Castillo saw that, in addition to the use of hot stones, blowing, and other native remedies, Cabeza de Vaca always said a simple prayer for healing, accompanied by the sign of the cross, the Pater Noster, (the Lord's Prayer), and Ave Maria (the Hail Mary).[58]

As with the other people of the region, the custom of the two Malhado bands was such that, if a stranger came to live as a guest among them, he was assigned to a particular man, his wife, and children. At first, the Capoques may have thought the thirty-six naked men were going to stay only a few nights, so one large hut was built for them; later, each was presented to one family. As a guest, Cabeza de Vaca was given a share of the food, and he slept each night in or near the hut of his host. In exchange, he had to gather food and firewood and do other chores or risk getting into trouble.

When he stood to speak for the exhausted Europeans, who had returned to shore from their sunken barge, the Capoques perceived that Cabeza de Vaca was the chief of this band of foreigners. Thenceforth, he lived with Principal, the local chief, the one "that had" him, as he recorded, and no doubt learned the local language primarily from him. Cabeza de Vaca does not offer a favorable report of his mentor because Principal required him to dig for roots, which caused pain and blisters.[59] At this stage he still had the tender hands of a typical European. Later, he developed the leathery skin and body of the indigenous people and harvested with his bare hands, without batting an eye, hundreds of prickly pears with their many stinging thorns.

During the winter of 1528-29, in the midst of a viral sickness of the stomach that struck the entire population of the island, some of the Capoques began to suspect the chief of the guests was an enemy, who, with his companions, had brought on the epidemic for the purpose of murdering the local people one at a time.[60] To protect those who remained, the Capoque men wanted to kill Cabeza de Vaca and the other few who were still alive. Upon hearing this proposal Principal bravely resisted his fellows. If the foreigners were using this disease to destroy us, he asked, then why had many of them died of it also? Indicating he was indeed their chief, he commanded them to abandon the plan.

Early in the spring of 1529, the same Principal and his family took the royal treasurer across the bay and upstream Halls Creek to set up a village on the mainland, perhaps near the town of Hillcrest,

Texas, and there Cabeza de Vaca also fell ill. If the sickness were, as he recorded, so "great" that he abandoned "hope of life," he would not have been able to get water and food for himself. During those days or weeks of convalescence, someone must have done it for him. The best candidate is the same Principal, who, perhaps along with his wife and children, took care of him until he was well, again saving his life.

While there is abundant evidence of other kinds, the mere presence of a native community there in the early 1800s demonstrates the attractiveness of Galveston Island as the seasonal home of the two bands. Principal, the mentor of Cabeza de Vaca, may have been a forerunner of the Karankawas, (also spelled Carancahuas), encountered by Jean Lafitte when he arrived in 1817, for they were living on the southwestern portion. Some native people had been seen on the island in 1783 by Spanish navigators when they first charted the bay and named it in honor of Don Bernardo de Gálvez (1746-1786), the Spanish governor of Louisiana.[61] In 1818 Lafitte hammered the Karankawas in a battle over a native woman one of his men had taken. He drove them from the island, perhaps to the region along the eastern end of Matagorda Bay where the Deaguanes formerly lived. After Lafitte was compelled to leave Galveston in 1821, some of the Karankawas returned to live there and in nearby areas until the early 1850s.[62]

Alice W. Oliver, who as a child lived near the town of Matagorda with her family (1838-48) describes one group of these coastal people. Their lifestyle was similar, if not identical to, the Capoque people of Malhado who welcomed Cabeza de Vaca. Ms. Oliver witnessed how they still had *físicos* since one night when she was sick in bed, one came with a group to her father's house with some "good water," possibly a tea made with herbs, to make her well. Like the Capoques of Malhado, they used the bow and arrow to hunt deer and other wild game and to fish. They crossed the inlets and bays in single-log, dug-out canoes, set up huts that were partially uncovered on the leeward side, and always camped near fresh water and brushwood for nightly fires. Their men wore only a deerskin "waist cloth" and spent a lot of time "wading in the salt water" for oysters and roots and to spear fish or catch them with traps and nets.[63]

That Galveston Island itself, or its widest fifteen-mile segment, was home to indigenous people in the 1520s, such as those described by Cabeza de Vaca, is also indicated by archaeological digs at two sites on the southwest Capoque part of the island.[64] Robert A. Ricklis, supervised an excavation in 1992 at the Mitchell Ridge site on the southwest bank of Eckert Bayou. He found that native people were living on Galveston Island "during the years" of the appearance of the Spaniards (1528-1532) as well as earlier and later. Artifacts uncovered there included shell ornaments, whooping crane bone whistles, and primitive tools made of bone and stones. The archaeological findings meshed "remarkably well" with the observations of Cabeza de Vaca in *Los Naufragios*, including the presence of *físicos* or "curers" who were buried with honor. He also found that fishing "was an important part of the subsistence economy." The native people "spent the fall and winter on the island" and then "went to other parts." Their huts or tents were partly open and exposed. There was "a relatively high regard for children" and also "a relatively high status for males," all consistent with what Cabeza de Vaca tells us.[65] Although Davenport identified Folletts San Luis Peninsula as Malhado no such comparable archaeological evidence has been found there.

Alleging strangely that it was "three times too long," Davenport dismissed the notion that Galveston Island was Malhado. Cabeza de Vaca tells us it was about fifteen miles, or five leagues, from the southwest point to the northeast. Surely Davenport is not saying the island is now forty-five miles long! He also did not consider that, at the time, it was shorter than it had been in the historical period.[66] Since Cabeza de Vaca indicated that Malhado was fifteen miles (five leagues) long, its northeast end must have been near Ferry Road, and its southwest terminus was at or near the southern city limits of the town of Jamaica Beach. As is typical of barrier islands, over the ensuing nearly 300 years, the shorter landmass kept acquiring more silt and sand at its southwest end so as to eventually merge with a neighbor island.[67] Two other examples of this phenomenon are Alabama's Dauphin Island, which from the 1840s to the 1950s grew at its western end so as to more than double in length, and San Luis Island that also grew at its southwest tip until it joined Folletts Peninsula in 1935.

Galveston has been described as "a narrow strip of land ... averaging in width about one- and one-half miles, paralleling the southeastern coastline of Texas," which is consistent with the half league across referenced by Cabeza de Vaca.[68] Davenport's curious assertion that Galveston Island was "doubly too wide" to have been Malhado was based on taking a very small slice of the island at its widest part and then requiring Cabeza de Vaca to match it. Davenport also apparently used a mistaken measurement for the medieval Spanish league instead of the correct three miles.[69]

The Han and Capoque communities would not have lived each winter on Malhado unless up and down its length there were many trees to provide branches for light and heat at night. When the log raft landed on the island, Cabeza de Vaca sent Lope to climb a tree in a nearby grove where he ascertained the type of landmass.[70] To build several bonfires for warmth, the shivering Spaniards easily found enough fallen tree limbs.

Yet, by the time of the first recorded descriptions of Galveston Island, there were not many trees, especially northeast of the isthmus at Sweetwater Lake and Offatts Bayou.[71] Upon his arrival in the winter of 1840, Francis Sheridan observed there was "hardly a shrub visible" anywhere on the northeastern section.[72] By then, the island was "destitute of trees," he wrote, and had the "general appearance of a prairie" that is "covered" everywhere "with a luxuriant grass."[73]

Many of the trees had been taken out by the first Europeans to live there. Attracted by the trees and the fresh water available, a group of European privateers arrived in 1816 under Louis Michel Aury (circa 1788-1821), and the following year, Jean Lafitte (circa 1780-1830?) set up his new base there. To build his little city and to cook and keep warm in winter Lafitte needed branches and logs.

Any trees that remained probably were eliminated by storms. A direct hit can destroy almost everything on an island surface, as seen in September 1900, when the worst storm in recorded history slammed into the northeast portion of Galveston, wiping out trees, buildings, and everything else across a large swath of the island. Another storm also blew across in the late summer of 1817, and razed Lafitte's newly built town and no doubt uprooted many trees.

It appears that for thirty to fifty years prior to 1528, the island did not receive a direct hit from a hurricane, a situation which permitted trees to grow and flourish throughout. Whereas Folletts San Luis Peninsula is naturally a treeless grassy plain, Galveston Island will grow trees if left alone. Live oaks grew naturally on Galveston Island and thrived in the city during the historical period. In some of the undeveloped spaces to the southwest of 61st Street, there were still some scattered stands of fairly large, wild trees until 2008, when Hurricane Ike caused most of them to die.[74] A visit to the Nature Preserve at Lafitte's Cove, northeast of the state park, will still provide a glimpse of what much of Galveston Island looked like in 1528—it was covered with brush and trees.[75]

Pieces of archaeological evidence found at the archaeological sites at Jamaica Beach and Mitchell Ridge reveal that these areas were inhabited in the early 1500s and were, therefore, part of the fifteen miles of island length. This means that the last three-to-four miles at the northeast termination point of the longer island would not have been included in 1528. This northeast section that includes Old Fort San Jacinto was the "island behind" of the narratives.[76] In the 1520s, it was separated by sea water at about the point of the southernmost part of Ferry Road where the landmass narrows.[77] During the decades in which Galveston Island was extending at its southwestern end, this smaller isle was also growing at its southwestern tip; the inlet between gradually closed so that by 1816, the two parts were one since the smaller isle had joined the larger.[78]

Consistent with the narrative evidence about Malhado, Galveston Island sits parallel to the mainland; its lagoon was and is sufficiently deep and wide to require a vessel to cross at either end. The canoe's crossing distances over the bay to the mainland harmonizes with the record.[79] A shorter Galveston Island not only had space for two Amerindian bands; it was, especially during fall and winter, well suited for human habitation. Local residents could gather roots and catch fish.[80] Unlike the drier Folletts San Luis Peninsula, on Galveston from September through January, there is a comparatively high quantity of rain, which provided fresh water in small natural ponds and shallow artificial holes.[81] "Water for cooking," as Francis Sheridan observed in 1840, was available "by digging a few feet in any part of the island."[82] These facts tend to confirm the hypothesis that the *Isla de Malhado* was a shorter Galveston Island.[83]

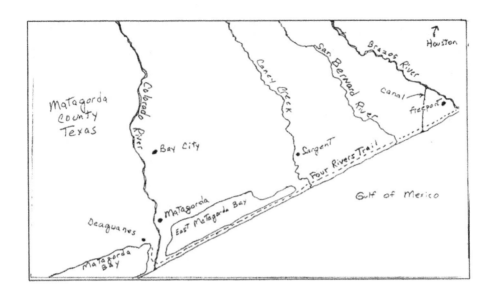

Map 3- THE FOUR RIVERS TRAIL. Dorantes left Cabeza de Vaca behind and led his group southwest down the shore. In transit, they crossed the mouths of the Brazos River, the San Bernard, Caney Creek, and the Texas Colorado River before taking a canoe ride over two large lagoons—Matagorda Bay and San Antonio Bay.

Chapter 4
Exploring the Lands between Houston and Austin

In the summer of 1532, under some trees near the Colorado River, in the area near Webberville, Texas, a barefoot, white-skinned man was warmly greeted by the brown-skinned native people when he arrived from the east. Álvar Nuñez Cabeza de Vaca was making his third solitary voyage as a traveling merchant and *físico*. The itinerant, bearded trader offered his seashells, cane sticks, and other "merchandise" for barter, and he tended to the sick one by one.[84]

"I had to remain with these same" native people "of the island for more than a year," he later wrote, which means he departed the Capoques in the spring of 1530.[85] Although he began his work of healing in 1529 at Malhado-Galveston Island, Cabeza de Vaca is silent in that he recorded nothing about his healing services during this period (1530-32). Further along, when narrating the great overland journey of 1535, he would have much more to say about it. Since he would not have stopped his curing prayers and practices for three years only to pick it up again, we conclude that he continued to offer the healing service during this period.[86]

Like the honored indigenous healers, he blew above the ill person or rubbed the area of pain, rituals he had learned on the island of Malhado, and that provided credibility with the local people. Similar in technique to European physicians, at times he took out his flint knife for surgeries or used a burning stick for cauterizations. Like the believer he was, over each patient he made the sign of the cross and, in Spanish, asked "God our Lord" to heal the person and to cause the people to treat him well so he could make a report about this unknown part of the world that would later become Texas and the United States.[87]

While Cabeza de Vaca was eager to search for New Spain, his friend Lope, the only other Spaniard still in the area, was not yet ready to travel. Somehow Lope seemed to know that there were people in those lands to the west who were unfriendly and capable of inflicting harm. He also was afraid of deep bays for he had never learned to swim. The royal treasurer must have been inwardly torn, for he, too, knew about large lagoons and mysterious forests to the southwest. What perils must he face if he trespassed into those regions?[88] On the other hand, instead of withering away in meaningless despair, he wanted to find a path out of the prison-like confines of Malhado-Galveston Island.

Fully aware of the dangers, Cabeza de Vaca renounced his fear and stepped into the abyss by boldly marching off alone in a search of an interior route to New Spain. In 1530, from the southwest end of a shorter Galveston Island, in the area of the town of Jamaica Beach, he crossed to the mainland and followed a path along Halls Creek to the village of Charruco, which probably sat near the bend in the Brazos River. Always pressing ahead to the west, he then passed among those who lived in *los montes*, his name for the dense forests along the Brazos, on a short segment of the San Bernard River and a long stretch of the Texas Colorado River.[89]

It is astonishing that he survived not only the first but also a second and a third solo journey deep into the wilderness of Texas. For eight-to-nine months per annum, in each of the years 1530, 1531, and 1532, he penetrated the interior on a great loop out and back again.[90] "I did not carry on my trade" in the lands of *los montes* "in winter," he later recorded, but instead he went back "to the island every year" to "beg" my compatriot Lope and to convince him "that we should get away the best we could" to "search" for the Europeans in New Spain.[91] Lope kept putting him off with promises to consider going "the next" year.[92]

If we were to stand on the shores of Halls Creek where the FM 2004 highway crosses, facing upstream west by northwest, we would see much the same scene as Cabeza de Vaca when he first hiked alone into the wilds. Departing on a sunny spring day, he likely saw large white clouds in a blue sky as he followed a native trail through green trees and brush that lined the river banks. Did he encounter alligators, red wolves, or puma lions? He tells us only that he faced many dangers and God saw him through.

Working his way up the Colorado River, he noticed that those who lived farther in were more hospitable than the Capoques on Malhado-Galveston Island, probably because they just gave him food and did not make him dig for roots. While he did not discover a route to New Spain, he came to be widely recognized as a trader and *físico*. He found that his merchandise and his healing services were the means by which he could safely travel from village to village. These years of exploration of the interior became for him a training course that enabled him later to lead his group on a long trek across the continent. Meanwhile, in addition to several of the regional idioms, Cabeza de Vaca acquired a common system of signs and gestures and a *lengua franca*, an oral language that was widely used.

In the years subsequent to the conquest (1519-21) of the Aztecs by Hernán Cortés, there were two attempts to establish colonies in the coastal areas of south Florida and South Carolina, and a few European ships had already passed along the Gulf and Atlantic coasts. However, prior to this expedition, no outsider had yet traveled into the inland regions of the United States. When the barefoot *conquistador* left the territory of the Capoques of Malhado, opposite the southwest end of a shorter Galveston Island, he became the first, along with his three later travel companions, to explore the interior of the United States west of the Mississippi and to survive, just as he had already been part of the first group to do so in the eastern part of the United States in Florida.

Since Spanish horses were not available in the lands of the U. S. until the 1600s, we can surmise that the Native American paths he traversed on foot mostly followed rivers or creeks.[93] The villages, as well as the trails of this era, were almost always close to fresh water, which they needed for drinking, washing, bathing, and cooking. In one of the early records of the indigenous people of coastal Texas, there is a description of how the men, first thing in the morning, ran to jump in the water - even in winter.[94] In places, the trails passed over dry areas from one stream to another, yet mostly in shorter spans of less than a typical single day's walk of eighteen to twenty miles. The Four Rivers Trail, for example, that went along the shore from Drum Bay to the eastern wing of Matagorda Bay provided fresh water for a traveler at the mouths of the rivers and creeks that came down to the sea at intervals along that path.[95]

The trees that grew along the banks provided another necessity, firewood in the form of fallen branches.[96] They "never settle with their houses" or huts "except where there is water and wood," Cabeza de Vaca recorded.[97] The people gathered dry tree limbs for their nightly fires on which they roasted venison and boiled roots or tuna pads in clay pots. Trees provided shade during hot summer days, firewood for light in the darkness, and cover in the event of an enemy attack.

Armed only with lessons in how to practice the healing arts and a shoulder-bag full of shells and canes, the royal treasurer mounted and followed existing footpaths that led him up to 150 miles from the shores opposite Galveston Island.[98] "What I wished to do most of all as I went about," to paraphrase what Cabeza de Vaca later wrote, "was to seek by what way I was to go later" on the journey to New Spain.[99] There was no creek that would have supported a native path due north, and he had no interest in crossing Galveston Bay to the northeast. Neither did he at first follow the route of

Dorantes down the shoreline to the southwest. Rather, he went *a la tierra adentro,* or inland, to the west by northwest from the region opposite the southwest part of the island.[100]

The beginning point of his yearly journey, for which he gave the estimated distance "from this island," was likely the canoe landing site on the mainland shore, possibly Carancahua Point, the promontory on the mainland shore opposite Jamaica Beach. From the area of the head of Halls Creek, the path would have crossed over to Mustang Bayou and then to Chocolate Bayou to follow each upstream in the direction of the bend in the Brazos River.[101] Departing Malhado each year in April, he would have stayed a few weeks in the land, or village, of Charruco, probably located in the region of the towns of Arcola, Missouri City, Sugarland, Fulshear, and Simonton, until he continued his exploratory journeys.

He hiked along a segment of the Brazos River valley in "the early days of spring, … the most beautiful season of the year …[when] oaks and hickories begin to show new growth. Redbuds, dogwoods, and magnolias splash the woods with pink and white blossoms. The prairies grow lush and green, soon to be blanketed with gaudy wildflowers. For a few weeks, nights remain cool while days grow warm with bright sunshine and brilliant blue skies."[102]

Although both accounts mention a voyage of 120 miles or 40 leagues "along the coast," this cannot mean that he traveled down the shore to Matagorda Bay, which from Galveston Island, would have been only some 70 miles.[103] Rather, these are inexact references to his first exploratory journey of about 120 miles *inland* at the farthest point before he turned back to the sea and then walked and waded northeast along the shore to Malhado. Feeling his way along in strange territory in his pioneer journey of exploration in 1530, he would not have ventured as far as he did in the subsequent two trips.

Upon reaching the area at which the upstream route turned sharply to the north, near the Texas town of Wallis, Cabeza de Vaca forded the Brazos River. Taking the shorter spans between rivers, he would have continued from there on a path, the San Bernard Trail, to meet and follow for a few miles the San Bernard River. Walking still farther to the west through the Atwater Prairie Chicken National Wildlife Refuge, he joined the trails that tracked the left bank of the Colorado River in the region between the Texas towns of Columbus and Eagle Lake. Since he suggests he visited multiple villages, we are not surprised that Native American artifacts have been found along the lower Texas Colorado River.[104] Having passed near the sites of the towns of La Grange and Smithville, on his second and third year of travel, to complete 140 to 160 miles, he went as far as Bastrop and the Lost Pines Forest.

If, as he says, he traveled "more than" 150 miles from Malhado-Galveston Island, it is likely that he reached Webberville just over the Travis County line. Since he saw no mountains during these years, he did not quite make it to the city of Austin. At about 180 miles it is a little too far and sits among the slopes at the edge of the Texas Hill Country.[105]

In October or November, to return to Malhado-Galveston, he reversed directions and mounted the Deaguanes Trail to go downstream, probably now on the right bank of the Colorado, to the region of its mouth near the eastern terminus of Matagorda Bay. Passing through or near the sites of Columbus, Wharton, Bay City, and Matagorda, he arrived at the two villages of the Deaguanes people. Since he describes a series of their battles, we surmise he spent considerable time there. On his final visit in the fall of 1532, he discovered that some of the local Deaguanes women were preparing to make a long journey by canoe.[106]

In each of these years, he traveled on a circuitous route that ended with a walk to the northeast on the Four Rivers Trail.[107] When the narratives tell us that three times he saw the great Matagorda Bay and three times he passed "along the coast," this refers to his return trips, southwest to northeast, which were made in the autumn of 1530, 1531, and 1532. Not having found an inland route, he now wished to go down the shoreline as had Dorantes, but he had not yet figured out how he and Lope could cross Matagorda Bay.

In the 1700s, Franciscan missionaries from the mission of *San Juan Bautista* in Coahuila, a few miles south of the Texas border town of Eagle Pass, traveled through these lands of *los montes* to their stations in East Texas.[108] In the 1820s, Stephen F. Austin brought immigrants to settle in this same area of the lower Colorado and the lower Brazos. In 1836, General Antonio López de Santa Ana and General Sam Houston crossed this region with their respective armies before they met at the Battle of San Jacinto. Over 300 years prior to 1845, when Texas became a state of the United States, Cabeza de Vaca lived in and explored these lands.

Within a generation of the publication in 1542 of the first edition of *Los Naufragios*, the British began to colonize in regions not yet occupied by the Spanish or the French. If they learned from *Los Naufragios* that there were "fruitful" places to live on this enormous continent, then Cabeza de Vaca made a major contribution to the migration of Europeans and Africans to the New World. Partly because of his book, English-speaking colonists knew to make landfall farther to the north in their attempt to establish colonies in what became North Carolina (1587), Virginia (1607), and Massachusetts (1620).[109]

Cabeza de Vaca, who always tells us about times of want, recorded little of it during these years except for those trips through the woods without a companion or guide between native villages that were at war with each other. The personal solitude itself was not a problem; he found in it a kind of refuge for renewal. Always near fresh water and carrying some food, from time to time he had to face storms and other perils as he wound his way through the woods.[110] On the San Bernard Trail going upstream on the left bank of the Texas Colorado River and on the Deaguanes Trail downstream on the right bank, he would have seen many deer, turkey, bison, duck, and raccoon; and, he may have encountered black bear, puma, alligator, jaguar, rattlesnake, and red wolves.[111]

He was privileged to see *los montes*, this region of the United States with its rivers, bays, hills, forests, and rolling grasslands, resplendent in unspoiled natural beauty. To him, though, without civilized European people, it was a "land, so deserted," full of wild animals, and with strange people living in small villages here and there along these creeks and rivers.[112]

He tells us that, during the "nearly six years" that he "was in that land," (actually it was nearly seven years), his scanty garb was the same as the native men, which would have been a native clout, a kind of belt and apron of deerskin or rabbit pelts that covered only the genitals. Nevertheless, Cabeza de Vaca considered himself to be "as naked as the day" he "was born."[113] According to Alice W. Oliver (1828-1889), who became well acquainted with the "Karankawa" people of the Texas coastal region in the 1840s, the men wore only a "waist cloth" or "a breechclout of skin," and the women wore nothing except "a skirt of deer skin."[114] European writers of this period, who did not consider such skimpy covering to be real clothing, frequently recorded that the native men and women were "naked." In the first days after the log barge broke and sank, he may well have been completely uncovered, but Cabeza de Vaca soon was dressed, as he put it, "*en cueros,*" in animal skins.[115]

Even after he arrived at European civilization in New Spain and was offered pants, shirt, and shoes, Cabeza de Vaca continued for some months to dress as he had during all those years. He recorded that he was "barefoot and naked," which meant barefoot, bareback, and minimally covered elsewhere. In Culiacán and everywhere he went during this time, he wore the same animal skins he had worn all along from Malhado to Corazones. An independent witness tells us that in July 1536, Cabeza de Vaca and the other three were observed entering the Catholic church in Mexico City "dressed in skins, just as they had [been when they first] arrived from the land of Florida."[116]

Although he referred to them as "lacking in reason and so crude in the manner of brutes" after the loss of the barge, Cabeza de Vaca had to accept his dependence on the local people for food, water, and safety. Clearly he became their friend.[117] Most of the European men of the expedition viewed the native people of North America, with their strange and primitive ways, as not much different from dangerous animals who should be avoided except when they had food or silver, or something else that could be stolen. It is perhaps illustrative of this attitude that five Spaniards, apparently from Dorantes' vessel, during the winter of 1528-29, refused to accept the lodgings, food, and water offered by the local Han band and stayed on the beach. One by one, they starved with the living feeding on the corpses until the last one died.[118]

Having learned to communicate with them and as a *físico* to serve them, Cabeza de Vaca set forth the case against brutality and in favor of "good treatment" of the indigenous people of the Americas. He observed that while some were hostile and merciless to their foreign guests and even to their own native children, others were friendly to the strangers from Europe and cared greatly for their children. The conquerors should deal with them hospitably, he argued. If so, most would gladly learn about European civilization and convert to the Christian God.[119]

When he finally arrived at the frontier of New Spain, in the coastal plain to the northwest of Culiacán, Cabeza de Vaca made a vain attempt to stop the "cruelty" with which Spanish slavers were, with impunity, arresting men, women, and children. Dragging them away in chains to sell as workers on Caribbean plantations and in silver mines, they were killing and torturing those who resisted. Although he was grateful to be back among Europeans, he told his monarch, he was filled with "sadness" to witness such malevolent behavior.[120] It was not the "sure road" that should be taken, he insisted; rather, the indigenous people "must be lifted up by good treatment."[121] The Spaniards should not "give any offense" against them "nor take their land from them but be their great friends."[122]

While the other three survivors had to endure, from 1529 to 1534, more than five years in a miserable state of servitude, Cabeza de Vaca himself was compelled to live this way only for a period of almost two years, 1532-34.[123] Contrary to what many of the books say, while exploring the lands of *los montes* (1530-32), he was a free man. To amplify and paraphrase what he wrote about his situation at that time:

"They treated me well and gave me food, out of regard for my merchandise. I had freedom to go where I wanted and was not a slave. Indeed, among them I was very well-known, and many wanted to see me. On those occasions of travel between villages when I was in the countryside and alone, I endured hardships that would be long in telling, as well as perils, hunger, storms, and cold weather. It was only through the great mercy of God our Lord that I survived."[124]

To justify his assertion that people who lived in the interior were friendly while those on the coast were cruel, he makes an ambiguous charge of "mistreatment" at the hands of the Capoques on Malhado. Nonetheless, apart from the fact that they forced him to dig for roots, they were reasonably hospitable to him. In the spring of 1530, when he departed as a trader and healer to explore the interior regions of *los montes*, they did not hinder him; indeed, they probably encouraged him. He likely would not have returned to winter each year with them on Malhado-Galveston Island unless they treated him well.[125]

On Malhado's beach when through his tears he saw the local men leaving, Cabeza de Vaca jumped up and went after them, and from that point, he affirmed the native people as real human beings; he learned how to live amicably with them. Without bullying them, without a sword or a horse, not demanding obedience or stealing their food or their minerals or their women, Cabeza de Vaca won their friendship. They taught him to be a *físico*, which became the key to success in leading his small group of survivors back to European civilization; he became as one of them and worked for their health and peace.

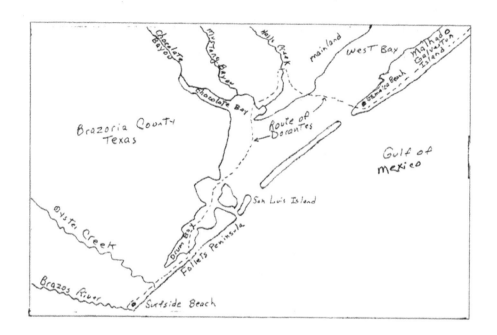

Map 4- DORANTES DEPARTS MALHADO. After they crossed West Bay in canoes, Dorantes and his group soon abandoned their search for Cabeza de Vaca; then they paid for a canoe ride over a second lagoon (Chocolate Bay) and the others to land about six miles northeast of the former Brazos River mouth.

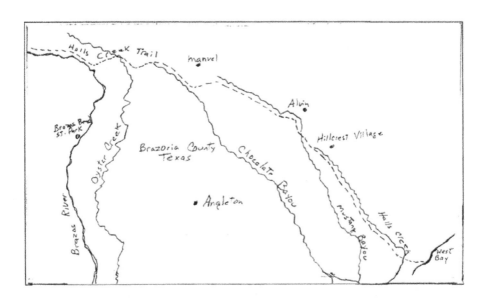

Map 5- THE HALLS CREEK TRAIL. In his search for New
Spain by means of an inland route, Cabeza de Vaca followed
existing trails alongside Halls Creek, Mustang Bayou, and Chocolate
Bayou before walking through the woods along the Brazos River.

Chapter 5
The Land of Pecan Trees
on the Guadalupe River

One morning in the fall of 1532, two bearded Spanish *conquistadores,* dressed only in a few pieces of animal skin, quarreled as they stood under some big pecan trees. There on the banks of the lower Guadalupe River, not far from where it empties into San Antonio Bay, Álvar Cabeza de Vaca entreated Lope de Oviedo not to depart. Years later he recalled how he "argued much with him that he should not" go back. Some native women were waiting for Lope beside a log canoe that was probably loaded with baskets of nuts.[126]

In the belief they could endure the dangers and find their way to civilization, he had, a few days before this, finally convinced Lope to join him on a search for New Spain. Cabeza de Vaca "took" Lope "out" of the Malhado-Galveston region on the same route followed years before by the Dorantes group. In a canoe, they passed over Chocolate Bay down to the landing site on the eastern shore of Drum Bay, five to six miles northeast of the former mouth of the Brazos River.[127]

After wading and walking along the coast the length of the Four Rivers Trail, he and Lope then went over the bay, or "the *ancon*" that now "was behind us," in another canoe with some women of the Deaguanes village.[128] From the region just north of the Texas

Colorado River mouth, they "crossed the bay," he recalled, referring to Matagorda Bay, combined in his mind with San Antonio Bay because they went over both in a single trip. The canoe ride was likely of two days duration with an overnight stay at the site of Port O'Connor.[129]

After they arrived at the pecan groves of Arboleda on the Guadalupe River, every day some of the local young men hit them with hands and sticks, or, with bows taut, they placed their arrows against their chests just to scare the two European men.[130] Confronted with the prospect of more of this kind of treatment, Lope wanted to go back to the Capoques of the Malhado-Galveston area where he felt safe and where he may have taken a wife.[131] Staying with the Capoques, he had to dig for roots, gather firewood, and carry loads, but he had gotten used to such a life, and he preferred it to taking risks.

The canoe slowly disappeared around a bend in the river. Now left behind, Cabeza de Vaca felt keenly the disappointment. He did not want to leave his friend to pass the remainder of his life under these conditions. Moreover, as far as he knew at the time, Lope was the only potential European travel companion still in the region. Turning his back on the bay that was part of the endless sea, he pivoted from gazing downstream to grimly face upstream and the long journey that was ahead. The footpath that was never far from the river led him deeper and deeper into the interior regions.

Lope returned home, and Cabeza de Vaca "remained alone" in this land he called "strange" and "desolate" that later became Texas and the United States.[132] Some local people had told him three other bearded foreigners had been seen and may soon arrive nearby; they attempted to pronounce their names, but it does not appear that Cabeza de Vaca knew who they were. Even if a few of the other Europeans of the expedition had survived until recently, in this enormous stretch of unknown territory, he knew there was no guarantee he would ever find them.

Only three or four weeks prior to the wrangle on the riverbanks, Cabeza de Vaca was traversing the Deaguanes Trail downstream the Texas Colorado River on his way back to Malhado-Galveston Island. When he arrived at one of the two Deaguanes villages, he offered his services and his "merchandise" as on his prior two annual visits.[133] He must have been startled to learn that some of the Deaguanes women were preparing to go by canoe *adelante,* or forward, to a forest on the far side of the big lagoon. At least twice before he stood at the eastern edge of Matagorda Bay, just south of the town of Matagorda, and looked wistfully across the water in the direction of the setting sun. He must have questioned to himself when, if ever, he would go that way to New Spain and from there to his European home.

Why were the native women making plans to travel to the woods of Arboleda near San Antonio Bay for a few days in fall when colder weather was coming?[134] It is likely that word had passed over the two large bays about the fruitful year in the pecan groves on the lower Guadalupe River. They were ready to take the two men across because while there they could pick up lots of the nuts to take back home. After asking the women to wait a few days, Cabeza de Vaca hurried up to Malhado and persuaded Lope to come with him.

In a canoe with the native women, Lope, and Cabeza de Vaca landed on "the other side" of the bay where the Guadalupe River flows into the northern end of San Antonio Bay, or Guadalupe Bay.[135] We know this because a few days after they arrived, they were about three miles from a place where other bands were coming for the many nuts that fell from "great trees" located "on the edge of that river."[136] Moreover, this site harmonizes with the purpose of the women in making this journey. If their men went to gather pecans for their families, they could be killed because they would be perceived as enemy combatants, but the women would not be bothered.

Although many of the trees have been cut down to build flood-control levees, and perhaps also for the prized timber, it is certain that from the 1530s to well into the 1900s, there were many pecan trees on the banks of the lower Guadalupe River. In the early 2000s, some of these trees still could be seen near the riverbanks at the city park in Victoria, Texas. Dr. L. J. Grauke, an expert on pecans, stated that historically there have been "beautiful groves of native pecans all along the Guadalupe River, almost all the way to its mouth at San Antonio Bay."[137]

After he was abandoned by his friend, the forlorn Cabeza de Vaca moped around under the big trees and crunched pecans as he pondered the prospect of a risky escape to travel alone to New Spain.[138] On the third day after the departure of Lope, a local man offered, probably out of respect for his healing services, to take him clandestinely only a few miles to the three other foreigners who had in fact arrived.[139] He was led to Dorantes, who was astonished to see he was still alive. They had not seen each other for almost four years, since about December 1528. This reunion of old friends in the fall of 1532 made it, Cabeza de Vaca tells us, "one of the happiest" days of his life.[140]

A little later, he greeted Esteban and Castillo, and together the four men passed many hours over several weeks catching up on all the news. When Castillo asked about his plans, Cabeza de Vaca responded unequivocally that he was going "to the land of the Christians," that is, to New Spain.[141] Dorantes interjected that he had been begging the others to "go forward" also, but Castillo and Esteban, neither of whom could swim, had hesitated because of rivers and bays.[142] The reference to salt water lagoons, *ancones,* indicates they were still planning to walk down the shore of the Gulf of Mexico to Pánuco and New Spain. However, the oppressive people with whom they now lived as slaves constituted, along with the bays, an enormous obstacle since they denied them liberty to leave.[143]

During the banter under the pecan trees, Dorantes recounted to Cabeza de Vaca all he had heard from Figueroa about how these people had killed most of their European companions from two of the Narváez expedition boats shortly after they landed, perhaps on San Jose Island. Hernando de Esquivel, who had described these events to Figueroa, was horrified to learn that native parents would kill their own children because of bad dreams, and there were occasions on which they threw a newborn baby girl to the dogs to avoid providing wives to their enemies.[144] One day, while Esquivel was living in this environment, a local woman announced that, in a dream the night before, she had seen him murder her boy. Poor Esquivel decided that to avoid a certain fate, he should flee, but he was chased down in the attempt and killed anyway. The native men who did it proudly showed Andrés Dorantes the sword, prayer beads, books, and other personal belongings of Esquivel.[145]

Their indigenous hosts wanted to keep them as slaves who were useful to gather firewood and do other chores. And two of them, Castillo now also, were respected physicians.[146] While the four Spaniards had some liberty to move about, at any time they could be commanded to go or come, to do this or that. Without permission, they could not move to join another band or even leave their individual host for another family within the band.[147] One of the European men was killed after their arrival in the region in 1528 just because he wanted to escape, and soon after the natives murdered a second Spaniard because he tried to change to another host-family within the community.[148]

In the conversations among the four men in the fall of 1532, the other three survivors were able to relate how they had gotten there. Some three-and-a half-years before Cabeza de Vaca and Lope arrived in Arboleda, Dorantes and his nine remaining men were taken across the two great bays by one or more of the Deaguanes people, who purposely landed on the east shore of Guadalupe Bay at the northern part of San Antonio Bay to avoid an encounter with the hostile people on the other side.[149] Since the Guadalupe River, with its fresh water, fish, and wild game was on the west shore, the Spaniards, who were weak, hungry, and thirsty, found themselves on the wrong side. Without enough food, several more soon died or were separated and never seen again. After some days, a native man gave them a little fish and took them across the bay.

For the next five and a half years (1529-34), Dorantes, Esteban, and Castillo, who had to submit to work and obey, were taken every year on a circuit to at least four distinct venues. They spent each summer in Nopales, a distant place of many prickly pears, or tunas, the pear-shaped fruit of the nopal cactus. The native people had such tough hands and tongues the prickly stickers did not hinder them. The thorny fruit, which they harvested and ate raw, provided sustenance for many people for at least three months each summer. The rest of the year was divided between Arboleda proper, the forested lands along the rivers with pecans in season, Refugio, a nearby grassy plain where they could hunt bison, and Aransas, a marsh full of deer and other wildlife with no rivers and almost surrounded by the sea and islands.

From the pecan groves on the lower Guadalupe, the native bands took their European slaves through the prairie grasses, roughly between the towns of Refugio and Austwell, down to the head of St. Charles Bay. This was a walk of about eighteen miles, six leagues *adelante,* or forward, which harmonizes exactly with the record. They arrived at "another bay," meaning St. Charles Bay, which separates Lamar Peninsula from swampy Aransas, or Blackjack Peninsula.[150] The latter has ponds with brackish water and is still populated by many deer, raccoon, turkey, alligator, bobcat, and other wildlife, including a multitude of pesky mosquitoes. Perfectly matching the evidence, both peninsulas are almost surrounded by sea water, and off the south and southeast shores of Blackjack Peninsula, there are many small islands as well as two large ones - San Jose Island and Matagorda Island.[151]

In his first visit to the region in April 1529, Dorantes fled his host band from somewhere toward the southern part of Lamar

Peninsula. This site is indicated because in his flight, he ran into another "great [body of] water," later known as Copano Bay.[152] From there, he turned back to hike across the grassy fields of Refugio and beyond to live with others that migrated along "the rivers," quite likely referring to Garcitas Creek and the lower Lavaca River.[153]

With shiny ponds and lush greenery, the land of Aransas, the winter home of the Whooping Crane, still is scenic and alive, yet the survivors said nothing favorable about it because of the living conditions. Cabeza de Vaca complained that in the early months of 1533, he and Dorantes suffered teary eyes "all night" as they tended damp-wood fires whose smoke kept mosquitoes away; if they went out to sleep on the west shore of San Antonio Bay, they were hit with sticks and ordered to return to the fires.[154] Adjacent to the eastern shoreline of Blackjack Peninsula, there is a long, narrow forest that provided firewood and is next to the beach. Hot sand here burned the feet of Castillo and Esteban in their earliest visit in the spring 1529 before their soles became tough like their native masters.

Undoubtedly Refugio, an extensive patch of prairie in the easternmost part of Refugio County, Texas, was one of three locations where Cabeza de Vaca saw large herds of bison.[155] "Cows come this far," he recalled, and the people "live off them" and make "robes" and "round shields" from the hides.[156] Unlike the marshes of Aransas to the south and the wooded rivers of Arboleda to the north, this flat patch of prairie in between provided succulent grasses for the bison to graze. Both then and now, it stretched out to the west from the shores of San Antonio Bay as far as the eye can see. In the fall, the local people set fire to these dry fields and thickets both to kill mosquitoes and to flush out lizards.

With a plentiful pecan harvest in the autumn of 1532, when the local people were relaxed about their slaves, they permitted the four Europeans to meet and talk after all chores were done. Careful to avoid revealing that they were discussing a plan to escape, this was an opportunity for the four to throw deerskin blankets over their shoulders as they sat around a bonfire at night. They would have conversed in Spanish, eating pecans, and warming themselves in the cold. The other three survivors saw that the optimistic Cabeza de Vaca was certain that, with God's help, he could find his way to New Spain, and they wanted to go with him. The issues now before them were how, from where, when, and in what manner they could safely get away.[157]

They wished to return to the seashore and go down it to Pánuco, near Tampico, at the edge of New Spain; however, there was no easy way to do this. If they went from the pecan groves south along the west side of San Antonio Bay, it would have led them to a kind of dead end since Blackjack Peninsula and Lamar Peninsula are nearly surrounded by water.[158] Castillo and Esteban could not swim. They had no canoe. The challenge was to find a route around all those bays, islands, swamps, and peninsulas and meet the sea farther down.

They needed some new ideas, and it may have been Cabeza de Vaca who proposed that the four should escape from a point well inland and away from the salt water. At a site some 90 to 150 miles to the west by northwest, they could turn south toward the sea to come upon Pánuco from the interior. At the very least, they would arrive at the seashore at a point significantly closer. In his travels in *los montes*, Álvar Cabeza de Vaca already had executed a maneuver of this sort three times from Malhado-Galveston, going around Chocolate Bay so as to intersect with the coast farther down.

But what trail would lead them to the west? Esteban, Dorantes, and Castillo had a ready answer. After they finish eating river fish at the end of May, all the bands in the region "begin to walk to eat the tunas" at Nopales, the land of many prickly pears, the fruit of the nopal cactus. They arrived after five-to-eight day trips on the Nopales Trail from the pecan groves on the lower Guadalupe River and stayed for up to four months. Most of the cacti are at the height of productivity in July and August and thereafter begin to decline. Yet, clearly, some of the fruit turned sweet in June, and others were still available in September or even in October.[159] If they broke away from the tuna fields to go due south, they could return to the seashore at a point farther down.

Cabeza de Vaca, who had learned in *los montes* how to travel from village to village, knew that in the first day or two on the path, they would need the assistance of a friendly group. Dorantes and Esteban had observed at Nopales a band, the Avavares, who seemed to be less inclined to make slaves of their guests. The Avavares arrived and departed each year at the western limits of Nopales, having come not from Arboleda to the southeast but from the lands of Los Rios to the south. They came up both for the prickly pears and to do business, bringing newly made bows and arrows to offer in trade.[160]

The four Spaniards would carry out this bold plot at the end of the summer tuna harvest just after the Avavares departed for the season.[161] The plan was to return to the seashore and then walk down the beach to New Spain. In September, their stomachs would be full of prickly pears and meat from the bison and other wild game that was so plentiful in the region of Nopales. Possibly, they could find some tunas in the field on the way and reach Pánuco by November.[162] After forming the secret plan between late November and mid-December 1532, the four had to wait six months to arrive at Nopales and then more than three months to put it into action.[163]

What if the only way, to break free to the south, required passing near a camp of their host bands? To this reasonable question, the other three would have had a quick response. At Nopales, most of the various bands set up their summer camps on or near the banks of the Medina-San Antonio River, which flowed roughly parallel to the meadows and hills to the south or west that were covered with the nopal cacti. If they made their escape to the south while out on the hillsides gathering the fruit, they would be moving away from the campsites. In this way, they could leave "without being noticed."[164]

If the problem of a traveler's gift came up, Cabeza de Vaca himself had the answer, for he alone of the four knew how important this was to the Native Americans when a stranger passed through their lands and ate their food. The other three Spaniards had not traveled freely since their arrival in Arboleda, and they had little or nothing with which to pay a host except their labor. Cabeza de Vaca had learned that his service with the healing rites and remedies acquired at Malhado was the best compensation, and here he taught Castillo to be a *físico* as well.[165]

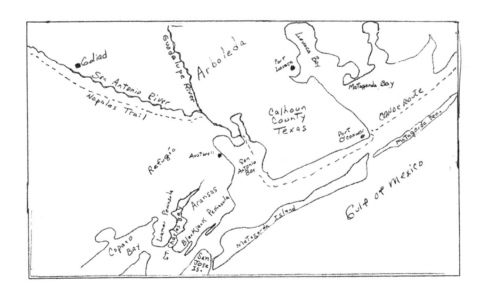

MAP 6 – THE LANDS OF ARBOLEDA, REFUGIO, AND ARANSAS. The Dorantes group, and later Cabeza de Vaca, found their way to Arboleda, the land of rivers and pecan trees. Their Native American hosts then took them to Refugio, a grassy plain where bison grazed and to Aransas, a swampy region adjacent to the sea.

Chapter 6
The Sojourn in the Region of San Antonio

At the end of the tuna season in September 1533, the four
survivors were about to carry out their dangerous plan to flee
into the wilderness. According to their scheme, they needed their
masters to lead them out into the hills only one more time so they
could make their move. Suddenly, the men of the Mariames band,
with whom Cabeza de Vaca and Dorantes had been living, started
fighting over "a woman."[166] Hitting each other with sticks and fists,
they barked angry commands and gathered their bags of dried fruit
and other possessions to go back east to their fall and winter
homelands.[167]

The Europeans had waited more than nine months for this
window to open, and then in a flash, it was closed. This season
there would be no flight to the regions beyond. Such a bad turn of
events would deflate even the optimistic faith of Cabeza de Vaca.
He could have gone alone since he knew how to travel solo among
the Native Americans, but he could not bring himself to abandon
his companions and chose instead to stay in these lands.

During the previous several months, while enduring periods of
hunger and many other hardships, at least he could talk to
Dorantes, since they lived with the same band, the Mariames.
However, Cabeza de Vaca soon had to run away from the
Mariames and thereby lost daily contact with his friend.[168] With

hope that they could make another try as he remembered, "In no way could we get together until [the] next year."[169]

In contrast to the amicable reception given him earlier by the native people of *los montes* and Malhado, the Mariames were so cruel he was compelled to search for a better situation. The barefoot *conquistador*, who may have been singled out because of his growing notoriety as a healer, later broke away to join a third and, finally, a fourth band. With each successive group, there were untold horrors and insults despite the fact that he was a respected *físico* who was frequently sought to tend to the sick.[170] Each time he escaped some of the native men ran after him to kill him before he joined another band.

That autumn, Cabeza de Vaca was not able to talk with the other three survivors about their plans while cracking and eating nuts. Unlike the year before, the great trees did not produce an abundant harvest in October and November 1533. Having not seen the others through the fall, winter, and spring, Cabeza de Vaca finally arrived, with his current host band, in June 1534 at Nopales; but he was not sure the other three were eager to implement the plot.[171] As the summer days drifted toward the end of the tuna season, he formed a strong conviction that if Dorantes, Esteban, and Castillo should flag in courage, this time he would leave without them.

From Arboleda on the lower Guadalupe River and from other places in the region, each spring the various bands started walking to Nopales, the land of many nopal cacti with their prickly pears, or tunas. At other times of the year, these groups were frequently at war with one another. Cabeza de Vaca describes fierce battles he witnessed in which some were killed, others injured. However, during the summer at Nopales, they all observed "the peace of the tunas." With plenty to eat during these summer months, the people stopped fighting and found occasion to socialize and trade for clay pots, fish nets, bows, flint rocks, arrows, deerskin blankets, red ochre (clay), or a spouse.[172] They also presented their sick to any curer or *físico* who was available.

Despite a set of definitive clues, both in the written record and on the ground, the precise location of Nopales has been unknown or misplaced – until now. The route of the four Europeans cannot be accurately traced unless we find this site, for it was from these fields of many prickly pears that they stepped into the unknown lands of south Texas to continue the long journey of survival.

To provide for the many native people for the summer at Nopales, the various native bands put up their huts at a place that was near a substantial stream with lots of trees. Their camps must have been located within a five-to-ten mile walk of some hills and meadows covered with nopal cacti.[173] Although they will grow almost anywhere, the prickly pear cactus thrives in higher areas where there is well-drained soil that is sandy and porous.[174] Those who went out to pick the tunas were not always near creeks for drinking water, we are told; this was because many of the cacti were up on the hillsides and away from the creeks.[175] During the day, the native people hiked into the hills to gather the tasty, sweet tunas, considered "the best delicacy they have," and in the afternoon, they returned to their camps near the fresh water. The tongues and hands of the native people, and now also of the four bearded strangers living among them, were so leathery they were not bothered by the sharp prickles when they handled and ate the raw fruit.

Since the tuna fields of Nopales are said to have been located "away from the salt water" of San Antonio Bay and the other coastal lagoons, the site must have been reached only after a journey inland of several days. Nopales was not at or near the Texas towns of Kingsville, in Kleberg County, as Davenport suggested, or Alice in Jim Wells County; each of these sites is too close to the Gulf of Mexico, and there are almost no hills or major creeks or rivers.[176]

To skip ahead briefly, the place of the prickly pears was sufficiently far north to be congruent with the half-day walk south to the Atascosa campsite of the Avavares upon their escape from slavery in September of 1534. It was a site also that fit with the subsequent five one-day trips taken to arrive at the Los Ríos Uno site on the Nueces River near where Cabeza de Vaca was lost for five days, which will be explained further along.[177] However, it was not so far north as to be in the small mountains of the Texas Hill Country because Cabeza de Vaca tells us he saw no mountains. Also, he suggests that in the land of Nopales there were few, if any, rocks.[178]

Along the San Antonio River, whose upstream course pointed from its mouth broadly west, the Nopales Trail led up to the Medina River mouth and beyond. Roughly parallel to the channel of the Medina-San Antonio River, which runs just south of and partly within the city of San Antonio, there is a row of connected green hills, thirty-plus miles in length, to the south and west.[179] Thinking of the measure to its nearest or easternmost part, from the area of the mouth of the San Antonio River, Cabeza de Vaca wrote that Nopales was some ninety miles, thirty leagues, distant, which corresponds with where the row of hills begins west of Floresville.[180] According to the other record, the hills extend *adelante*, or ahead, "more than" 120 miles, forty leagues, to the westernmost reaches in the area of Somerset.[181]

On this elevated divide between two river basins there are many sandy, well-drained meadows. It was the perfect place for the prickly pear cactus to thrive. Due to clearing for homes, farms, and ranches, there are not as many as in the 1530s. Still, in the early 2000s there were many cacti, especially of the black nopal, whose ripe fruit is dark red or purple.[182] If left alone the land would produce multiple times more as it once did.[183]

By putting up their campsites near the Medina River, scattered at intervals roughly between the overpasses of Interstate 35 and 37, or the San Antonio River, between Interstate 37 and State Highway 97, each day the native people could walk south or southwest into the meadows and hills to gather the tunas and each afternoon return to their camps to socialize, trade, drink water, and spend the night.[184] The reference to the "rivers" reflects the author's memory of several tributary streams that pour into the main channel, including the uppermost part of the San Antonio River and Leon Creek.[185]

The campsites were set up under the thick canopy of trees that, still in the twenty-first century, covered both banks of the Medina-San Antonio River and provided fallen branches for the nightly fires as well as shade on hot summer days for the people of the 1500s. As much a part of daily life as electricity came to be later for the residents of San Antonio, the nightly campfires provided warmth and light and facilitated socializing, tending to children, and community activities.[186]

To the native people of the age, for whom a five-mile walk was a mere stroll, the Medina-San Antonio River was reasonably close to the tuna-covered hills to the south and west. The people would have been content to walk this distance twice each day to harvest the fruit. However, they could not cover the full length of thirty-plus miles of this place from a single spot. During the summer at Nopales, the people were "never settled," Cabeza de Vaca tells us, because every few days the camp was moved to be near more of the ripe fruit.[187]

To take home the fruit each day, saving some for later consumption and to give to children and the elderly, the people put the prickly pears in *seras* or animal-skin panniers "like Europeans do with figs." They "keep them to eat on the way when they return; and they grind the peelings and make them into powder."[188] Later, at Los Rios Dos, a second place of many such cacti, Cabeza de Vaca was presented a *sera* full of fruit after he prayed for a deceased man.[189]

The local people did not bring along heavy clay pots full of water into the fields of harvest; they could not easily bear the weight of both, that is, a *sera* full of prickly pears and a pot of water. To quench thirst when not near a creek, they drank the juice of tunas that had been squeezed into a hole. When they were out in the hills, they "lacked other vessels," we are told.[190] They had clay pots at home for various uses, but instead of carrying "others," *otras*, they slung their *seras* over their shoulders.[191]

The "lovely meadows" mentioned by Cabeza de Vaca are still seen in many places in the country just south of the city of San Antonio, which was built, in large part, on a swath of the Blackland Prairie on the upper San Antonio River.[192] Here many lush green tracts covered with cacti and succulent grasses stand in contrast to the rugged terrain of the Texas Hill Country to the north and the arid scrubland to the south.

Cabeza de Vaca recorded that the people ate "nothing but" the prickly pears. However, on occasion they surely had wild game, including bison.[193] Cabeza de Vaca saw many of the "buffalo," and he was the first eyewitness to write a description.[194] The principals of a Spanish expedition that went through the area in 1691 were astonished by the size of the bison herds they saw.[195] After European missionaries and other Spanish-speaking settlers had been living there for over eighty years, there were still large numbers of bison in the fields around San Antonio. In the early 1800s, a "semi-annual slaughter of buffaloes ... [took] place in the months of May and October."[196]

It is a "very fruitful land" and would be, Cabeza de Vaca said, an ideal place for "civilized people" to inhabit.[197] Based on his observations during his sojourn in the area in 1533-34, he predicted that the "fine pastures" he saw in the region of San Antonio and just to the south also would be a good site for cattle ranches.[198] In fulfillment of his prescient words, beginning in the early 1700s, farms for breeding cattle were established there by Franciscan missionaries and their cohorts. Spanish-speaking Native Americans and *mestizos* who worked on these sites were the first "cowboys." The cattle that the Franciscans brought across the Rio Grande formed the main strain of the Texas Longhorn breed.[199]

These few bright words of commendation about the San Antonio region are striking since his experience in the region was otherwise negative and perilous. The references to "beautiful meadows" and "very fine pastures" stand out in a dreary story of slavery, dangers, and "great hardships."[200] Cabeza de Vaca would not have so described Davenport's choice for Nopales, in Kleberg County, whose terrain is flat, dry, and uninteresting. Having unearthed prehistoric relics in the San Antonio region, archaeologists have noted that with its "slow-moving water, pecan trees and wildlife," not to mention the prickly pears, the area was, in fact, an "ancient paradise for indigenous people."[201]

His description of the land upon which the city of San Antonio was built is congruent with what others saw.[202] In June 1691, Domingo Terán de los Ríos (late 1600s-early 1700s), the first governor of the Spanish province of Texas, and Franciscan missionary Damián Manzanet (late 1600s-early 1700s) saw that it was a "very beautiful" part of the country with "low hills," rivers that contained good water, some heavily wooded areas, and also many grassy fields.[203] In 1709, Pedro de Aguirre, along with Father Isidor de Espinosa, another Franciscan missionary, commented on its large trees, "good ground," and bubbling, fresh water.[204] Upon returning in 1716, Espinosa saw lots of prickly pear cacti, some of which were "very tall."[205]

Although they did not realize Cabeza de Vaca had spent time in the region (1533-34), the Franciscan missionaries who founded (1718-1720) the two original missions that became the city of San Antonio had an opportunity to read Cabeza de Vaca's book *Los Naufragios*. From it, they gained an interest in traveling north from Querétaro in New Spain to, and beyond, the great river to work among the indigenous people described therein.[206] The Franciscans may have seen an affinity between Francis of Assisi, Giovanni Francesco di Bernardone (1181-1226), the founder of their order, and Cabeza de Vaca, both of whom were deeply spiritual and spent time going about "barefoot" and almost naked while ministering to the sick and the poor.

While Cabeza de Vaca appreciated the natural beauty of the region, he still wanted to carry out the clandestine plan to get out of there and on the road home again. According to the plot, at the agreed hour on the chosen day, each of the four was to make his way separately and secretly to a well-known place they expected to be unoccupied because all the tunas there had been picked. The rendezvous may have been a notable hill located well to the west at a point in the season when most of the bands were migrating to the east. Since Alonso de Leon tells us the four passed southbound near the site of Cerralvo in Nuevo Leon, it is clear that, from the rendezvous in Nopales, near San Antonio, they marched roughly due south.[207]

In a desire to return to the Gulf of Mexico and go down its shore to Pánuco and New Spain, it appears that the four Spaniards were thinking, wrongly, that the Gulf shoreline continued at the same angle they had traveled along the beach southwest from Malhado-Galveston Island. They were unaware that beginning at San Antonio Bay, the coast turns sharply due south.[208] Traveling on a course due south from the west end of Nopales near Somerset, they were moving, not as they thought, so as to intersect with the shoreline, perhaps it would be near the Texas town of Hebbronville, but rather parallel to it.[209]

At Nopales in the summer of 1534, Castillo rejoined Dorantes and Esteban, who were living with a different band, and these three agreed that the long-awaited escape plan would be carried out "after Cabeza de Vaca arrived."[210] Cabeza de Vaca also went up, and in late August or early September, he met the other three. At "the time of the tunas" we "came together again," he reflected, and we "agreed to flee."[211] Later on the very day that they finalized the plan to depart a few days hence, their hosts began to move the campsites so as to separate the four Spaniards, an act which could have ruined everything the same as the year before.[212]

The royal treasurer had pondered the possibility that something like this may happen to again block them, and he was mentally prepared to make the escape, at least for himself, without further delays. He seized a brief opportunity to tell the other three in their secret language that on the day following the next full moon, he was going to depart the region. If between now and then, he stated unequivocally, they were not able to see each other to confirm the details, he would break away to the rendezvous point, and, with or without them, travel south. To paraphrase how Cabeza de Vaca expressed it:

"Before the other three went away with their host bands, I told them I would wait for them in the tuna fields [i.e. in Nopales] until the day following the next full moon, and I informed them that if on that day they did not come [to the meeting place] as agreed, I would go alone and leave them."[213]

While Cabeza de Vaca was watching for the full moon and "waiting ahead," or to the west, the two groups with whom the other three were staying then moved to the east and put up their camps opposite a part of Nopales where the cacti had lots of ripe fruit that had not been taken.[214] As the period of daylight gradually diminishes and the temperature begins to drop, September in Texas is typically a time of rapid transition. With the full moon deadline approaching for Dorantes, Esteban, and Castillo, the situation was beginning to be urgent. With fewer and fewer tunas available, all the native groups were sure to soon leave.

Some "three or four days" after the separation, the other three were able to get together; they decided "to search for Cabeza de Vaca."[215] Desperately trying to find a way to somehow join their true captain before he departed, they came up with the idea of an attempt to go to the campsite of his host band under the ruse of a mere visit to retrieve him. Almost at nightfall they pointed to some columns of smoke in the distance and indicated they wished to "bring" Cabeza de Vaca "there in their company."[216]

Since Cabeza de Vaca was a famous *físico*, he would have been highly valued as a guest-slave by any of the native groups. Probably because Castillo was now also a *físico*, he was not permitted to go.

Only Dorantes and Esteban were granted a few days to go look for Cabeza de Vaca. So intent were they to find him, the two departed immediately and walked "all night" in the direction of the columns of smoke. In transit they got lost and had to ask for assistance from a man who, presumably the following morning, "took them where Cabeza de Vaca was."[217]

With the night of the full moon drawing near, this host band, now with Cabeza de Vaca, Dorantes, and Esteban, once again moved their camp. The new site, while probably still on the Medina River, was farther to the east, and, as it turned out, quite close to that of the host band of Castillo. For a day or two, all four of the Spaniards could again meet in the evening and pick fruit near one another during the day.[218] Almost two years had passed since they formed the plot under the pecan trees on the banks of the lower Guadalupe River. They knew well that to avoid being killed, they must execute their secret plan to perfection. According to the moonpage.com website, there was a full moon on September 21 that year, which means the day of escape was probably September 22, 1534.[219]

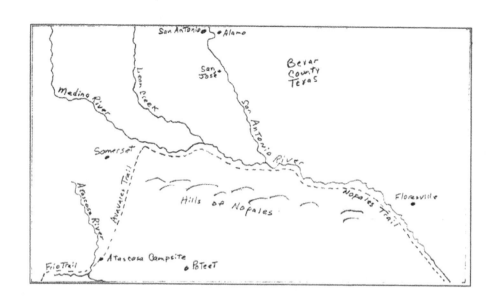

Map 7– NOPALES, THE REGION OF MANY PRICKLY
PEARS. Covered with prickly pear cacti, the hills of Nopales lay
between Somerset and Floresville, and the native camp huts were
put up along the Medina River and the San Antonio River.
Typically, each day the people walked several miles south or west to
harvest the tunas.

Chapter 7
Lost on the Nueces River

On the morning of the escape, Cabeza de Vaca and his three companions strolled for the last time among the huts and smoky remains of bonfires under some large, bald cypress trees near the banks of the gurgling Medina River. As on previous mornings in Nopales, they walked with their host bands south four-to-six miles away from the villages in the forest. They could have arrived within a couple of hours at the cacti-covered hills and meadows.[220]

The plan called for the four to split up and, when completely out of sight, to leave individually and "secretly" from various places. Subtly, but steadily, Cabeza de Vaca made his way out into the fields until he was "separated [and] by himself."[221] Furtively watching to be aware of anyone nearby, he began to pick tunas, eating some, bagging others as if it were a normal day. Although eager to break away, he had to avoid doing anything that would draw attention to himself. When all was clear, he could stop pretending to be merely gathering fruit. Now he could start working his way west through the cacti and the tall grass.[222]

The record says that the four men commended "themselves to our Lord," and considered "it was best" not to continue "to live such a savage life and so distant from the service of God and of all good reason, …and [so]… they left."[223] Around mid-day Dorantes, the first to arrive at the rendezvous, stopped and saw, as expected,

72

no one was there because all the cacti in the area had already been stripped clean of the tunas.[224] Within minutes, the others walked up to this place, in or near the Texas town of Somerset, toward the western terminus of Nopales and far from the other bands that were moving to the east. Cabeza de Vaca and his companions then quietly turned south toward the sea, or so they thought, on a seven- or-eight hour walk on the Avavares Trail.[225]

Wearing only animal-skin clouts and their shoulder panniers, the four unarmed men, now without guides, stepped into the vast scrubland of South Texas. Through weeds and thorny shrubs, they marched, not really knowing what was ahead. Sometimes they could see the path and sometimes not. Nearly two years before, under the pecan trees of Arboleda, they had discussed the danger. They knew that, with all the uncertainties, they were taking a big risk; but they had to do it. They would never return to civilization unless they escaped and fled into the open country.

In fear of being discovered, at first they walked silently and rapidly. After about three hours they worried less about getting caught by those behind and more about whether they would find, before nightfall, those ahead.[226] Scanning the horizon for any sign of the Avavares, in the distance, they saw, just as the sun was setting, columns of smoke rising above some trees. Was it the camp for which they were looking? Would the people of this band make slaves of the four escapees and treat them badly as the others had? It was getting dark, and they were not sure they could find the campsite.

Then, in the fields not far away, they saw a man. He bolted in fear. To try to catch up with him, Cabeza de Vaca sent Esteban, the slave of Dorantes and the first person of African descent to live in the United States. He had spent more than six and a half years in Texas (1528-1535), long before the first African slaves arrived at Virginia in 1619. Esteban, the black Spaniard, who was adept at learning languages and hand signs, was greeted warmly by the

Avavares man who recognized him as one of the bearded foreigners seen back at Nopales.[227]

The man guided them to a campsite that must have been in the area where Farm to Market Road 2504 passes over the Atascosa River. This was the only stream in the area large enough to provide the necessary water and trees. If the camp were located near the Texas town of Rossville, it was, for the Avavares, about a one-day walk of fourteen to eighteen miles south from the Medina River, and, for the Spaniards, a half-day walk of eight to twelve miles from the crest of hills in the region of Somerset.[228]

Using hand signs, the royal treasurer told the Avavares they had been searching for them. Later, when he inquired as to where their fall and winter homelands lay, the Avavares pointed downstream due south along the Frio Trail that ran parallel to the uppermost Atascosa River. This was just the direction the Spaniards wanted to go. They would not have traveled with the Avavares west or east. From this time forward, the four accepted invitations to go to other places only if the proposed direction of travel was "farther ahead and more pertinent to their way and intention."[229]

Thinking that by going south they were on the way to the sea, the four men passed through these hot, dry lands where hunter-gatherer groups lived along the Nueces River, the Frio River, the Atascosa River, and San Miguel Creek. Archaeological excavations on the Frio River in 1977-82, at sites later covered by the Choke Canyon Reservoir, unearthed arrow points, pottery, scrapers, and many other artifacts. These findings confirm that Native American groups lived along these rivers in the 1500s, as well as before and after.[230]

On the night they arrived, those of another band came down the riverside path to request the curing services of—not Cabeza de Vaca but—Castillo.[231] Why did they not ask for Cabeza de Vaca who had been active as a healer-physician all the while from his initiation on Malhado in 1529?[232] Clearly, Castillo had built his own reputation after observing Cabeza de Vaca when he arrived at

Arboleda in the fall of 1532. That he learned from Cabeza de Vaca is indicated by a casual reference to an incident that occurred later at Los Rios Dos. There, at a second place of many tunas, Castillo refused a request to tend to a man who was almost dead. In such difficult cases, Castillo "believed that his sins would hinder the cure from always turning out well."[233]

Had Castillo learned the healing arts directly from the Native Americans, he likely would not have made the prayers for healing its main instrument and his sins a possible impediment. He picked it up from Cabeza de Vaca, who had blended Christian petitions with indigenous rites and practices. At about this time, Esteban and Dorantes also became *físicos* in the style of Cabeza de Vaca, possibly because the Avavares mistakenly assumed they already were. The Avavares chief assigned Esteban and Dorantes to hosts who were *físicos*, as if they were physicians, although the two had not yet begun to perform the curing rites.[234]

They expected to spend a few days with the Avavares and then continue their journey south to the sea. However, when the Avavares warned them about icy conditions beyond their homelands, they decided to stay with them until spring.[235] Having already passed through several frigid Texas winters of the "little ice age," the Spaniards took the caution seriously.[236]

Since the Avavares were skilled makers of bows and arrows, the four naturally supposed they would employ their fine weapons to provide deer, turkey, rabbit, and other game. This impression was reinforced when that first night the Avavares gave them pieces of tasty roasted venison. Members of other nearby bands walked up and, as honorarium for the healing services, offered them even more food.

Moreover, the Avavares at first did not demand that their guests earn their keep by obedient labor and submission. Proud that these well-known *físicos* were living with them, they permitted the physicians to visit the ill in other communities nearby. The Spaniards began to feel content, not only had they finally escaped the brutal slavery of their former hosts to the north and east, but they also had an easy ticket to pass through the coming winter and spring.[237]

Their assumptions did not prove to be true. The sojourn with the Avavares in 1534-35 was a stage of progression from slavery to liberty but not yet to celebrity and prosperity. The eight months spent with the Avavares turned out to be another difficult ordeal. Later in the season, the Avavares commanded Cabeza de Vaca and the others to do menial tasks such as tanning deerskins and gathering firewood. Even worse, in the winter and spring the Avavares refused to go hunting for their hungry guests. On the rare occasions when meat was available, the native men were permitted to steal it just before the Europeans put it in their mouths. Even the usually confident Cabeza de Vaca at times lost his positive outlook and was discouraged and forlorn. While looking at the blood coming from cuts he sustained from the thorns and bushes as he gathered firewood in thickets, he began to doubt that he would ever emerge from this "captivity" in these "strange" lands. He later reflected:

"When I found myself [trying to deal with my bleeding wounds and other hardships, there was] no other remedy or consolation except to think on the passion of our Redeemer Jesus Christ and on the blood which he poured out for me, and to consider how much more serious was the torture that he suffered from the thorns, than that which I was then undergoing."[238]

At the end of a journey of five one-day trips from the Atascosa campsite, with little or nothing to eat, the Spaniards crossed to a different stream. We "arrived at a river," *un río*, "where we set up our lodges," Cabeza de Vaca later wrote, using the singular; yet there were places in the region he described as being among "the rivers," *los ríos*, using the plural.[239] The area of the Highway 16 bridge over the Nueces River is strikingly congruent with these references to both a "river" and the "rivers." A few miles to the east downstream and at other places farther upstream, there are long segments at which the river divides into two or three channels. Still other creeks pour into the river from both banks so that, on this part of *the* river, especially in that wetter age, there were several *rivers*. All three of the main Avavares campsites in the fall, winter, and spring of 1534-35 were on one and the same waterway, the Nueces River.

While we cannot ascertain all the details of the journey to the Nueces River, plausibly, on the first travel day, the Avavares led the four Spaniards south eighteen to twenty miles on the Atascosa River and then to the southwest to San Miguel Creek, west of Goldfinch in Frio County. From an overnight camp there, they trekked seventeen-to-nineteen miles on the second day downstream the Frio River east of the Texas town of Dilley. In two more travel days of eighteen-to-twenty miles down the Frio, they passed near the village of Fowlerton to a point a few miles west of the town of Tilden.[240]

After the Europeans made the half-day jaunt of eight-to-ten miles south from the Frio to arrive mid afternoon at Los Rios Uno on the Nueces, there was enough daylight left to look for food. With some of the Avavares and his three companions, Cabeza de Vaca worked his way east and downstream through this region that was mostly covered with grasses, cacti, and scrub brush. They were looking for mesquite trees that grew in places here and there, along with small live oak, post oak, and ash. Especially near the rivers and streams, the mesquite trees could be found with their pods that contained little beans. Cabeza de Vaca wandered off alone in a riparian grove of these larger trees. Several hours later, under the dense leafy canopy, he did not notice that the sun had almost set. At nightfall, he finally turned around and was seized with fear when he realized the others had gone back to the camp, thinking he had as well.[241]

When he attempted to get his bearing and follow his companions, he found this forest confusing. All around there were "rivers" and "many trees." He saw no trails and could not find the main channel. The darkness and the chilly air were gathering around him. He did not have time to sort out the "rivers" and find his way out. Even though he had no deerskin blankets, he would have to spend the night alone right there. The remains of a natural fire caught his eye. A nearby tree was still hot. He could recline near it to keep warm through the cold October night. If he survived until daylight, he could find the others; surely they would wait for him.

When morning came, the barefoot *conquistador* began his lonely journey. While he had never been in this region, he knew which direction to go to find the Avavares and his European companions. They were on their way to Los Ríos Dos, another site with many tunas where "people of other nations and languages" camped in October and engaged in social interaction similar to Nopales, although on a smaller scale. Without wasting any time speculating on where they might have gone, Cabeza de Vaca took up the correct path along the Nueces River.

In LaSalle County, fifty to sixty miles farther upstream to the west from the Highway 16 crossing, a distance that harmonizes perfectly with the narrative, there are some hills. Near the town of Cotulla where President Lyndon B. Johnson once was a school teacher, two-to-four miles from the left bank of the Nueces River, the hills rise to about 500 feet in elevation. This was Los Ríos Dos, the second place of an abundance of prickly pears.

Having survived the night near the simmering tree, the next morning Cabeza de Vaca came upon the Los Ríos Uno campsite that had been occupied a few hours earlier and was now abandoned. If he hoped to meet a rescue party, he was disappointed. The Avavares and the Spaniards could have waited a few hours, but they did not. Along with Castillo, who was several years his junior, and Esteban, who dared not challenge his owner, Dorantes later excused himself as being too weak and hungry to wait or to go look for their lost leader; he gave him up for dead as he had once before.

Cabeza de Vaca was far from dead. Just as he had done on the beach at Malhado-Galveston and on those occasions when he was alone in the deep forests of *los montes* along the Colorado River, he looked for a way to keep living. He had a persistent confidence that eventually, however long it may take, whatever troubles must be faced, with God's help, he would make it back to civilization and to his home in Europe.

Meanwhile, the Avavares broke camp on that first day after arrival and started moving upstream. At about the same time, Cabeza de Vaca began walking upstream also, but slowly because his feet were bleeding. Also, to be sure he would have a campfire each night he was carrying an armful of sticks, some of which were burning. He made only twelve-to-fifteen miles of progress each day instead of the usual eighteen-to-twenty. He alone and they together were traveling the same trail in the same direction.

On the second evening, wearing only his animal skins, Cabeza de Vaca knelt at a small clearing near the river and scraped out a shallow pit. Truly afraid of the cold of the night, he gathered dry branches for firewood and some bunches of tall grass to use as both cover and cot. Desperately clinging to life and praying often, he curled up on the ground between four bonfires and slept in the cross-shaped depression he had dug.

When morning came, he pressed on, doggedly making his way upstream. Although he had attained the tough soles of a Native American, his feet were still bare and vulnerable. He "shed much blood" from them.[242] At the end of the third day, and the fourth, he still had not found his fellow travelers. While it was a severe test of body and spirit, he hinted that such difficulties were an opportunity for meditation. Perhaps for him there was a connection between prayer and solitary walking. "The slamming down of the feet, the being at one with myself, landscape, and God, tiredness, the mind shutting up and stilling," as one has observed, "walking, pilgrimage itself, became prayer."[243]

Each long dreary night he battled the cold by reclining between the flames. Once he had to jump up from sleep because his hair caught fire. Finally at the end of the fifth day, he happily found the Avavares group and his three travel companions at Los Ríos Dos on "the bank of a river," the Nueces.[244] This site was near the hills of cacti, for on the night of his arrival, they offered him some tunas they had already picked, and the next day, they all walked out to gather more. Once again, he had been delivered from the valley of the shadow of death.

After the Avavares finished harvesting tunas at Los Ríos Dos, now in early November, they returned downstream to Los Ríos Tres, the final seasonal campsite. From here the four Spaniards departed the next spring of 1535. Congruent with the southbound pass near Cerralvo, Los Ríos Tres must have been located near the mouth of Ygnacio Creek on the Nueces River.[245]

As he traveled from band to band through the wilds of Texas and northern Mexico, Cabeza de Vaca, who attributed all aspects of his survival to divine mercy, was teaching the indigenous people about the creator God. We know from the records of the Francisco de Ibarra expedition of 1565-66 that the native "Querechos" honorably remembered Cabeza de Vaca, not only because of the cures, but also because of the instruction they received. They looked up and stretched out their arms to pray because, it appears, they had learned from Cabeza de Vaca that God above was the one who made the sun and all things, and he alone should be worshipped.

During the sojourn in the lands of Los Ríos, the four were told of visits of a demon from hell, the *mala cosa*, who had appeared in years past, wounding and frightening the Avavares. At first laughing it off as a silly joke, Cabeza de Vaca eventually became convinced that something real had happened, and he responded with a little sermon:

"If you will believe in God our Lord and be Christians like us, you need not have fear of that one, nor will he … come to do these things [again], and you may be sure that as long as we are in the land he will not dare to appear in it."[246]

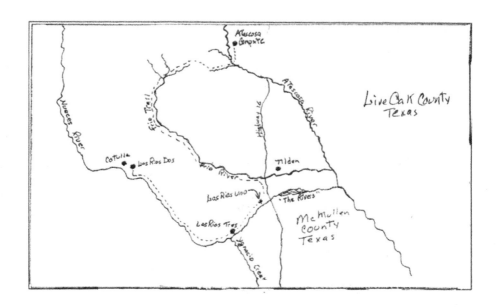

Map 8- THE FRIO TRAIL AND THE LANDS OF LOS RIOS.
From the Atascosa campsite, the Avavares led them along the Frio
Trail to Los Rios Uno, a few miles from where Cabeza de Vaca got
lost among "the rivers." After five days he finally caught up with
the others at Los Rios Dos near Cotulla.

Chapter 8
The Adulation of Cincuenta
in Far South Texas

When, in the spring of 1535, the time came for the four to begin walking twenty miles a day on the trails to New Spain, none was physically ready.[247] Since the Avavares, with whom they lived, gave them only small amounts of food, they had barely survived the colder months. On many days there was nothing to eat. All four were thin and weak. Cabeza de Vaca described how the Native Americans searched for "whatever [food] they can get."

He said, "Occasionally they kill some deer, and at times they take some fish, but this is so little and their hunger so great that they eat spiders, ant eggs, worms, lizards, salamanders, snakes and vipers that kill those they bite, … they eat earth and wood . … the dung of deer and other things which I refrain from telling; I believe, truthfully, that if in that land there had been rocks, they would eat them as well."[248]

In these lands along the Nueces River, there was an abundance of deer, turkey, rabbit, and other game, but the Avavares rarely went hunting. The Spaniards did not hunt for themselves, probably because they could be mistaken for enemy combatants. The bows and arrows tendered to them as gifts were used only for barter.[249]

Despite his physical weakness and hunger, his fear of dying by starvation in the country ahead, or of being made a slave again by another indigenous community, Cabeza de Vaca was eager to get started. Esteban was ready also, but not Dorantes or Castillo. About eight months earlier, to goad the others into carrying out the escape plan, the royal treasurer had threatened to leave alone. Would Cabeza de Vaca have to do it again? He knew there was no future in lingering with the Avavares at Los Rios Tres on the Nueces River.

If Cabeza de Vaca issued a summons to commence the journey to the seashore, Captain Dorantes rejected it, preferring to stay with the younger Castillo until a friendly band and some food were found by someone else. Aware that the long odyssey would begin with the first few steps, the royal treasurer marched away one morning upstream Ygnacio Creek taking with him the willing Esteban.[250] Since their hosts had not yet gone north to Nopales, it was likely in late May that they, as the record says, "started walking."[251] It would be a long hike.

To reach the Rio Grande, the Spaniards traveled approximately 135 miles over the next few weeks in a series of seven trips of one day or less.[252] On a southbound course roughly parallel to the hills of the Reynosa Plateau to the west, they trekked across the rugged lands of Duval County and Jim Hogg County, working their way through shrubs, cacti, mesquite, and other small trees.[253] The starving men looked hungrily at many prickly pears as they passed, without eating any because they were still hard and bitter.

On the first travel day, Cabeza de Vaca and Esteban hiked about twenty-one miles, or a typical one-day walking distance.[254] At mid-afternoon, the two men arrived at the friendly village of the Maliacones, likely on Rosita Creek just to the southeast of the Texas town of Freer. Here they were offered green mesquite beans, the "small fruit of a tree," which burned their mouths and left them thirsty.[255] It was not much, but the Spaniards were so hungry, they would have eaten almost anything. Wasting two days, poor Esteban had to go back to fetch Dorantes and Castillo with word that some food and friendly people were ahead.

With all four men together again, they departed the village of Maliacones aiming to go due south to the sea and then down the shore to Pánuco. The trails they followed were in proximity to the few small streams of this dry region. On the way to the village of Arbadaos, they stopped to gather more mesquite beans, which made this a shorter jaunt of perhaps fifteen miles. Arbadaos could have been near the Texas town of Benavides on the southeast-flowing Santa Gertrudis Creek.[256]

Those of the Arbadaos band, which was divided into two villages, were hospitable, but they had even less to eat than the Maliacones. These sickly people did not bring in any game to roast and offered only tiny amounts of water, yet the Spaniards stayed eight days. Perhaps the famished Dorantes, just as he had been reluctant to leave the Avavares to start walking the trails, refused to go any further; it appears that he saw no future in continuing to march into the unknown wilderness.[257]

Cabeza de Vaca, the erstwhile merchant, may have been the one who remembered that poor as they were, they had acquired a few things of value. With a deerskin and some nets, the desperately hungry men purchased two dogs from the Arbadaos people, which they roasted and consumed. As a result, they regained sufficient strength to renew the journey and were shown the way to Arbadaos Dos, the second village of the community located "near" the first.[258] Marking the third travel day, this short walk, probably about six miles, was likely to the southeast flowing Aqua Poquita Creek, a tributary of Los Olmos Creek of Duval County.

Following the Ygnacio Trail roughly parallel to Highways 359 and 16 between the Texas towns of Benavides and Randado, they took leave of the weeping people of Arbadaos Dos who were grieving at their departure. If Cincuenta, the village of fifty huts, is accurately placed a few miles south of the tiny Texas village of Guerra, the four Spaniards persevered without native guides over longer-than-normal distances of twenty-nine to thirty-three miles on each of the next two travel days, the fourth and fifth in sequence.[259]

On the fourth day, finding no people, little food, and a "lack of water," they resumed the journey through this region in which the terrain and the flora rendered it "rugged and impassable."[260] Among the thorny shrubs, nopal cacti, and sage, they followed a small path that may have been a game trail. Then, finally, they witnessed a providential smile in the form of an all-day downpour. The showers filled the creek beds from which they frequently took a drink.[261]

Walking in the rain after completing about eighteen miles, they entered a large thicket in which they lost the trail. Another favor was granted when they came upon a patch of nopal cacti. Here they gathered, not the prickly pears that were still mostly hard and bitter, but a large quantity of the padded, green, oval-shaped "tuna leaves," or stems.[262] The cactus stems were held until later when, at sundown, after walking another ten to twelve miles, they camped alone, probably on Baluarte Creek, several miles south of the town of Hebbronville. Despite the wet conditions, they found some sticks and made a bonfire in a hole in which they cooked the stems all night.[263]

On the fifth travel day, they had a hefty breakfast of the pungent cactus stems that had been baked into a softer and more palatable state. Still in the thicket, and lost, they started again. With the heavy rain of the previous day, they found plenty of fresh water to drink in the small, east-flowing streams. Yet, like runners at the twenty-mile point of a marathon, they became weaker and weaker. The Spaniards had fallen into a despair in which many would abandon hope, sit under a tree, and wait to die. What to do now? Their leader wanted to continue, so they kept going, pushing ever deeper into the wilderness—to the south, to the sea, or so they thought—and eventually to Pánuco and New Spain, they hoped.

In southwest Jim Hogg County, Texas, as the sun was setting, they ascended the watershed that separates the basin of the Nueces

River from that of the Rio Grande.[264] They found a trail again. Suddenly, out beyond them, there were two women and some children who ran away to hide behind trees. When the Europeans coaxed them "by signs," they slowly approached, trembling.[265] No, they had no food. Yes, they would guide the four travelers to the village.[266] The Spaniards had been searching for a band, but they had no idea what the people of the village would do when they walked up.[267]

Finally, "that night," the four weary ones "arrived at the settlement where there were fifty dwellings." These Coahuiltecan "wiki-up" homes have been described as "small circular huts with frames of four bent poles … covered with woven mats."[268] The men wore an apron-like "waist cloth," and the women nothing except a skirt of grass or animal skins. The village of Cincuenta was a dirt-poor community, but it was also the site of a turning point. Here the native people "first began to fear and reverence" the four Spaniards and "to esteem them much."[269]

The settlement must have been on the south-flowing Remadura de Charco Largo Creek at about the Starr County line, a site that fits with De Leon's evidence for a southbound pass near Cerralvo.[270] In the early 2000s, this little gully, one of very few creeks in the area, was dry most of the year, but in that wetter age, it carried a steady stream of water that sustained two hunter-gatherer communities. From here, the water runs down into the great river southeast of Rio Grande City where it is called the Los Olmos Creek of Starr County.[271]

Historian Harbert Davenport, who misidentified the island of Malhado and promulgated a number of other errors about the journey, also set forth the myth that the four *físicos* emerged from the barren wilderness as "strong holy men . . . marching triumphantly from tribe to tribe."[272] Not yet. After the long trek that followed their unhappy sojourn among the Avavares, who abused them and sent them away malnourished, the bedraggled wanderers were neither strong nor triumphant. Feeble in body and soul, they were not sure what would happen next.

At first, the people of the community were frightened of the four strangers who had appeared out of the uninhabited lands to the north. When they realized they could come close without harm, they gathered around. Although weary with fatigue, Álvar Cabeza de Vaca was amused that these brown, beardless men and their wives and children, upon seeing that one was black and three white, wanted to touch their faces and beards, perhaps to be certain they were real![273]

While his three companions may have been hesitant to offer anew their healing services, since it appears to have won them few favors among the Avavares, Cabeza de Vaca was ready. He remembered that at various times back at Arboleda and Nopales, at least some of the natives had shown deep appreciation for the healing services. Since these of Cincuenta, the village of fifty huts, had no acquaintance whatever with them, he wanted to promptly notify them that they were *físicos*. Using hand signs, Cabeza de Vaca introduced himself, possibly something like this:

"We request some food and a safe place to stay for a few days before we continue our travels. I am a físico. Tomorrow, if you have any who are sick, you may bring them to me. My three companions are also physicians."

Allowed to rest for the night, they were confronted the next morning by the same crowd who were now waiting for them to fulfill their promised services. All the people, who at first had been terrified of the strangers, now were begging for a blessing and were presenting sick friends and family to be cured. With a multitude gawking, the four went to work, surely for hours, dealing with their patients one by one. They ascertained the condition of each individual sick person and focused their attention on the appropriate part of the anatomy. Still weak from the near starvation of the prior months, they almost did not have the strength to say the prayers. They were barely able to lift their hands to make the sign of the cross, not to mention to do the rubbing and blowing expected of *curadores*, or healers.[274]

To the people of Cincuenta, the village of fifty huts, and those of nearby Cincuenta Sur, these unarmed strangers were a marvel. Guided by their leader, the four "were not greedy for anything" and freely attempted to alleviate suffering.[275] Each took time to deal with the sick one at a time, asking only for something to eat and a safe place to sleep in return.

The Avavares had ordered the Spaniards to make deerskin mats, dig for roots, and gather firewood; when a little meat was available, they had permitted their fellows to steal it from their hands, and, worst of all, refused to provide enough sustenance.[276] In contrast, beginning at this remote village in the scrub country of far South Texas, the native people began to revere Cabeza de Vaca and the others as if they were visiting royalty. No longer were they lowly, abused beggars. Now they were honored princes whose every need must be met. Of vital importance, they were given more food, although at first it was just roasted green tunas and cactus stems. Because there was plenty to eat, they elected to stay for two weeks to regain lost strength and weight. The four healers were taken completely by surprise at all the gifts and attention. How different this was from the treatment they received in previous years as slaves in Arboleda and Nopales!

At first, they thought only these two villages would lavish such favors upon them. As nice as it was, they had to brace themselves to face other native communities that would not be so hospitable. Some days later, farther down the trail, they made the happy discovery that this highly favorable treatment would likely follow them from village to village along the route. This spirit of adulation was picked up and carried, not by the four Spaniards, but by native runners and guides. The word passed from village to village down the long line of connected trails from South Texas to the region near the west coast of Sonora, Mexico, and beyond. The attitude of the native people toward Cabeza de Vaca and the other three was the same as in the place it began when, several months later, they reached the village of Corazones in the Pacific coastal region.

Cabeza de Vaca said, "We never cured anyone who did not say that he was better."[277] His meaning seems to have been that at certain places everyone for whom they offered their services and rites claimed to be better. The record mentions rubbing, blowing, praying, as well as making the sign of the cross for the sick and injured. The *fisicos* also employed herbal teas, hot stones (or heat therapy), cauterizations, and surgeries, which were standard medical practices. Denying that the healing rites and practices occurred at all, there are some who allege the accounts of ministry to the sick are false tales. All of it was, they say, fabricated to sell more books, gain political appointments or impress church officials.[278]

From the time of their pass through Cincuenta in South Texas until they arrived in New Spain, the Native Americans gave the four extraordinary acclaim, food, many favors, and gifts. If they were not offering the healing rites as they moved through, why did the native people treat them with such deference? They did not dote on Coronado this way, or even on the Franciscan missionaries who later went into New Mexico and Texas. Long years afterward, various indigenous groups who lived in widely separated localities voluntarily gave highly favorable reports about the good works, including the attention to the ill and the marvelous cures wrought, in connection with the visit of Cabeza de Vaca and his party.[279]

To regain strength, the Spaniards lingered about two weeks at Cincuenta and for another few days at nearby Cincuenta Sur. Meanwhile some of the local residents reported to other villages what was going on. Hearing about wonderful instances of healing and restoration, those of Calabaza, the village of gourds, sent two women with gifts and an invitation for the four *curadores*. On the night they arrived, they received the summons at Cincuenta Sur, where the custom was to eat mesquite beans with a handful of muddy clay from a pit. Yes, the European men ate such food and gave thanks for it! This village sat on the same Remadura de Charco

Largo-Los Olmos Creek, about six miles south of Cincuenta and that much closer to the Rio Grande.

After the *físicos* ascertained that Calabaza was located farther to the south, they decided to depart the next day; but the local leaders "begged" them "greatly" to wait one more day so the two women could rest. Although they made the trip in a single day, the village was "far away," they said, and the four would need guides since the Calabaza Trail was not easy to follow.[280] The next morning the women were not permitted to go with them. Once again the four men walked alone. Had they lost the adulation that started at Cincuenta?

The travelers started out on this long, one-day trek going south along the downstream route of the Remadura-Los Olmos Creek, but they did not go to its mouth on the great river. Since we know they passed southbound near Cerralvo in Mexico, the path must have connected to *another* south-flowing stream.[281] The evidence indicates the trail to Calabaza followed a creek that poured into the Rio Grande within a few miles of the Río El Alamo mouth near Ciudad Mier, Tamaulipus.[282] If the *físicos* had crossed the Rio Grande at the Remadura-Los Olmos mouth southeast of Rio Grande City, or at any point further downstream, they would not have been close to the El Alamo mouth and not in a logical position to make a pass on trails that followed streams near Cerralvo "from the north."[283]

Had they continued downstream the Remadura-Los Olmos Creek, they would not have gotten lost in transit, as both narratives mention they "soon" did. Not long after their departure, they reached the mouth of a tributary stream and nearby there was a second creek mouth. At the turn from going downstream south to upstream west on El Chapote Creek, they were confused. Of the two branches which one to follow? When they stopped for a drink, after going a short distance farther upstream, the two native women from Calabaza suddenly appeared. With two more women from Cincuenta Sur, they had somehow broken free of the authorities.

Their stop at the turn to discuss the puzzling situation is telling. If they were following the same creek downstream to its mouth on the great river, they need only to have glanced at the water from time to time to be sure they were going with the flow. To turn upstream when there are two or more tributary options, as there were here, is a different matter.[284] They followed the El Chapote and a tributary, the Los Barrosos Creek, to its head, or source, and then hiked over a short distance to the head of the Arroyo La Minita.[285]

Cabeza de Vaca and his companions crossed the great river when it was "already late in the afternoon," and later "at sunset" they reached Calabaza, the village of gourds.[286] The record says, "they walked that day eight or nine long leagues without stopping all day," and "before the sun set, they arrived at a river."[287] After going twenty-five-to-thirty miles just to reach the Rio Grande, they then trudged another few miles to the village on the Río El Alamo.[288] To be consistent with the reference in De Leon and with the hypothesis that the pathways tended to follow the fresh water of creeks and rivers, the Calabaza Trail they took must have run the full length of the Arroyo La Minita down to its mouth on the Rio Grande.[289]

From this point in the journey, they were frequently surrounded by adoring women in a culture in which *físicos* could have as many wives as they wished and where indigenous men thought little of lending out their own wives.[290] Beginning with the explosion of adulation at the two villages in South Texas, the indigenous people presented various gifts and favors. This may have included their sisters, daughters, and even their spouses. A couple of incidents occurred after the conclusion of this journey that support this inference.

On the Marcos De Niza expedition in 1539, Esteban appeared to retain an expectation that he would receive the same sexual favors as in 1535. He made demands for the young women of a Zuni village in western New Mexico. However, Esteban was no longer under the leadership of the generous and devout Cabeza de Vaca, and the Pueblo people knew nothing of Cincuenta and had no special regard for this stranger. Tragically, they killed him.

Camped in Blanco Canyon in West Texas in 1541 with a band of bison-hunting "Querechos," men of the Coronado party saw an interesting female, *una india*. In a brown-skinned, indigenous community, this girl was distinctly white and reminded at least one of the men of the pale, smooth skin of the noble women of Castile. More than likely, she was about five years old and was the daughter of Dorantes, Castillo, or Cabeza de Vaca. Some six years earlier, the four Spaniards had spent four or five days traveling through the Trans Pecos Texas region with the mother and her band.[291]

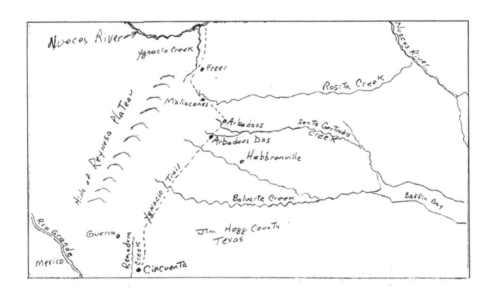

Map 9- THE YGNACIO TRAIL. From Los Rios Tres (the
Avavares winter-spring campsite on the Nueces River), they
traveled south on the Ygnacio Trail through the villages of
Maliacones, Arbadaos and Arbadaos Dos before a two-day trek to
Cincuenta on the south-flowing Remadura de Charco Largo Creek.

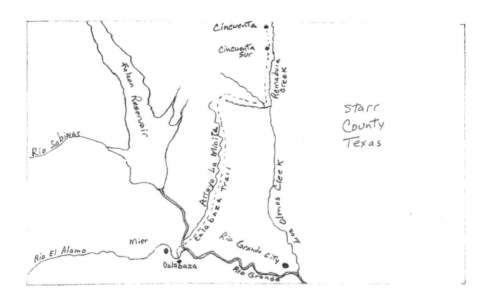

Map 10- THE CALABAZA TRAIL. From the village of Cincuenta Sur, they followed the Calabaza Trail south along the creek before turning west upstream one of its tributaries (where they got lost) and then down the full length of the Arroyo La Minita to the first crossing of the Rio Grande.

Chapter 9
The Turn Inland

The four men stood with the native women among the lush green trees and brush on the Texas bank of the great river. Cabeza de Vaca saw that the waterway was about the width of the Guadalquivír at Seville (150-200 feet). Even in late afternoon, the July sun was still high in the sky. Bright rays were shining in their faces and on the immense volume of blue water that flowed south to their left.[292] Monarch butterflies that migrate through this region may have been flitting around the greenery on both sides along with Altamira orioles and other exotic birds. "When evening had already come," Cabeza de Vaca later recorded, "we crossed a river … whose water was chest deep."[293]

Álvar Cabeza de Vaca and his three traveling companions were the first non-natives to see this majestic river.[294] Recalling the second of three times they waded across, he described it as "a great river that was coming from the north," *un gran río que venia del norte*. On the third time, he noted it was a very large river, *un río muy grande*. In Mexico, its name is Río Bravo del Norte. In the United States, it is the Rio Grande, as he called it.[295]

They were on the way to Calabaza, the village of gourds on the Mexico side, whose inhabitants had heard animated tales about the four strangers. They marveled upon hearing that, out of the wilderness, the four strangers had appeared at Cincuenta, the village of fifty huts, on the Texas side to offer their services for the sick

96

and injured. Two Calabaza women were sent across the river to find these men. When they arrived at the village of Cincuenta Sur, they saw how, during a "great celebration," the four were highly venerated. The women presented gifts and invited them to Calabaza, their home village. Upon discovering that this village was farther to the south, Cabeza de Vaca and the others departed alone the next day.

While the two women wanted to accompany the four to Calabaza, they had to wait for permission. After the first few hours of hiking alone, the Spaniards got lost, but the native women caught up and guided them the rest of the way.[296] Farther along, a man from Calabaza met them on the trail and, after walking with them a while, he ran ahead and waded across the river to announce their arrival. All the people of the village, men, women, and children were now waiting anxiously.

Powerful swift currents made crossing the great river neither easy nor without danger.[297] If Esteban and Castillo hesitated to step in, since neither could swim, Cabeza de Vaca would have reassured them. Earlier in the journey, he had made clear that, if one of them succumbed, he would pull him up and across. Holding aloft their panniers, the Europeans and their women guides slowly worked their way over the great river.

On the far side, they continued walking for another hour or so, until it was almost dark.[298] Just at nightfall, a noisy crowd suddenly surrounded them shouting loudly, slapping their legs, and shaking dry gourds, *calabazas,* with pebbles inside.[299] Pushing and shoving in the twilight, they all wanted to touch the four famous physicians. "They nearly killed us!" Cabeza de Vaca later reflected.[300] Then they lifted their guests and carried them the rest of the way, crossing the shallow Río El Alamo in the process. Although the *físicos* were tired and sleepy, the people passed the entire night in "songs and dances" around the campfires.[301]

Still, at this stage, the four were trying to understand what was going on in relation to the indigenous people. After years of being shamed, insulted, and mistreated as slaves, they were still not sure what this favorable attention meant. Would it continue down the trail? Should they try to take advantage of it? Should they linger in the region for another year or so? No, they would eat, sleep, pay their respects, tend to their patients, and hope for the best as they continued the journey.

To locate Calabaza and this segment of the route, we are assisted by Alonso De León the elder (d. 1661?), who traveled extensively in the region in the early 1600s.[302] He recorded a tiny but crucial fact that has been ignored too long. The local indigenous people remembered this to De León about the visit of the Cabeza de Vaca party in 1535.[303]

"[Now I present a word] in regard to what Cabeza de Vaca did and concerning the works that transpired with him and his three companions as they were on the journey of Pánfilo de Narváez in and through the land of Florida [including Texas and the whole Gulf Coast region]. They crossed the land from over there [on the Gulf Coast] to the South Sea [or the Pacific Ocean/Gulf of California]. As they went, they were teaching the primitive people that lived here [in Nuevo Leon and Tamaulipus in northeastern Mexico]. Through the virtue [or power] of the sign of the cross, they were also doing for them [the native people] many miracles [of healing] to the extent of reviving the dead. .... and it appears, by [the use of] a sound rule of cosmography [or navigation], from where they left [in order] to arrive at the place where they arrived, [at the lower Río Yaqui] they were forced to make a passage through and very close to the site where today [about 1639] sits the town of Cerralvo. They passed [near Cerralvo] from the north."[304]

This paragraph of De León points like an arrow to the approximate site for Calabaza, the village of the clamorous welcome with gourds and to the place at which the Spaniards first saw the Rio Grande. To be in position to make a southbound pass near Cerralvo in Nuevo Leon, after they forded the great river, the trail followed upstream the Río El Alamo and its tributaries. The huts of Calabaza sat in the vicinity of Ciudad Mier in Tamaulipus, Mexico, on the banks of the El Alamo, a short distance from its mouth.[305]

Because they kept going for a while after wading across, it is apparent they traveled down the Arroyo La Minita to its mouth. This is the only stream that flows from the north to form a connection with tributaries of the Remadura de Charco Largo Creek and whose mouth is just the right distance from that of the Río El Alamo. On this trail the four were "forced," as De León indicates, to continue southbound. They were under the impression that they could not turn west until they reached the southern tip of the Sierras.[306]

After all the commotion subsided, after the all-night "songs and dances," and after the sick were treated, Cabeza de Vaca knew they must try to find out where they were in relation to the North Sea, the Gulf of Mexico. Part of the escape plan was to go south from Nopales to circumvent the bays that lay to the southwest of the marshes of Aransas. They thought they would meet the sea earlier, at about the site of Hebbronville. Unknown to them, the Texas shoreline, starting at about San Antonio Bay, bends sharply and eventually points due south, not to the southwest.

From the region of Somerset southwest of downtown San Antonio to Calabaza near Mier and then to Cerralvo, the line of travel indicates a change of thinking at Calabaza. From there the logical route would have been to follow the Rio Grande down the right bank to the ocean and then along the beach to Pánuco near Tampico. Instead, they turned west and southwest to move away from the sea. This evidence tells us that at Calabaza they formed a new plan by which they would go to the coastal region, not of the North Sea, the Gulf of Mexico, but of the South Sea, the Gulf of California, and they would walk each day as far as possible without any long delays.

Why did they turn inland at Calabaza? Cabeza de Vaca undoubtedly held to the mistaken notion that the distance to the west coast was not too far. He must have known that, subsequent to the conquest of Tenochtitlán in 1521, Hernán Cortés established a Spanish presence on the Pacific coast near Acapulco.[307] On the route there from Veracruz through Mexico City, it was about 500 miles. Cabeza de Vaca did not know that to arrive at the Pacific coastal plain near Ciudad Obregón, it would take them more than three times that measure, and they would still be over a thousand miles from Mexico City!

The barefoot *conquistador* seems to have had an esoteric attraction to the distant regions that lay west of the Texas coast, as if he felt it was his destiny to penetrate those "far away" lands. He wanted to go home, but he also wanted to explore unknown places. Unaware of an enormous desert to negotiate, it appeared to him that, in the interior, there was more food and fresh water. However, the most important reason for this decision to turn inland was that the people who lived north of Pánuco were "very bad."[308] The *físicos* "did not want to go" on to Pánuco "because they had taken warning ... [not to go there] .... and for these reasons they wanted to go higher [inland]."[309]

In the early 1600s, Europeans who migrated to the region of Tamaulipus and easternmost Nuevo Leon described the indigenous bands who lived there as "wild" and "completely savage" because they engaged in barbaric practices such as eating the flesh of the dead.[310] In 1554, only nineteen years after this journey, when a Spanish ship wrecked on South Padre Island, these native people killed about 100 European survivors who were trying to walk down the beach to Pánuco and New Spain.

In the secret European language, the four huddled to discuss these stern warnings. They had no knowledge of the geography of northern Mexico or Trans Pecos Texas. They did not know if they could trust everything the local people were telling them. Nonetheless, they wasted no time in changing travel plans. If they could not approach New Spain in south-central Mexico from the east coast, they would go to the west.[311] Cabeza de Vaca and the other three decided it would be "better to go across the country" to explore unknown regions.[312] "If God our Lord would be pleased to save [even] one of us," he later wrote, "… he could give important information to others on his return to civilization."[313]

From Calabaza, the Cerralvo Trail led them through several, well-populated villages, past the site of Cerralvo and on to Platita, the village of silver, whose features are so clear as to render its approximate whereabouts one of the more nearly certain locations in this part of the journey. Platita was located in proximity to a mountain in which there was silver ore; we infer this from the fact that they presented the Spaniards "some small bags of silver" nuggets.[314] Also, it sat near the "point" of a range of mountains, or where they "begin," and in a region where many people lived.[315] Here, the local people insisted that they go not "inland," or west, upstream a nearby creek but south to a village at the foot of some different mountains on a route to the sea.[316]

The vicinity of Los Ramones in Nuevo Leon is near "the point," or the southernmost end of the line of the Sierra Papagayos. It also sits close to the Río Pesqueria, a creek which, when followed upstream, leads inland broadly to the west and then around to the other side of the chain of mountains on a trajectory to the northwest.[317] If they would follow the Bustamante Trail that tracks "that river," they were undoubtedly told, although a long distance over multiple trail segments, it would eventually take them to the sea on the far Pacific side of the continent. In the 1570s in the nearby Sierra de Los Picachos, other Europeans discovered silver.

Just as the four physicians in 1535 met many people on the road who stopped them to request attention and blessings, European slavers who entered the region in the 1570s also met multitudes of Amerindians whom they perceived as candidates, or victims, to seize and make slaves.[318] Alberto del Canto (1547-1611) appears to have been the first European, subsequent to the party of Cabeza de Vaca, to travel into greater Cerralvo in 1576 or 1577, and Luis de Carvajal y Cueva (1539-1595) came soon thereafter.[319]

Tragically, some of the children of the area who welcomed the European Cabeza de Vaca in 1535 with festive celebrations may have been, in the 1570s and 1580s, arrested illegally by the European Carvajal after greeting him gleefully on the false assumption that, like Cabeza de Vaca, he would be a generous servant. The cruel confiscation of the indigenous people, who were sold as slaves to work in mines and on plantations, stands in sharp contrast to the acts of the gentle peacemaker who went through offering hope to the sick and injured.

With their discovery of silver and also lead in the mountains of the Sierra Los Picachos, Canto and Carvajal began the process that culminated in the construction in 1582, of the mine called San Gregorio and the mining town of Cerralvo, which served for a while as the capital of the state of Nuevo Leon.[320] The gift presented by the Platita people of little bags of silver nuggets and the fact that, forty-seven years later, European entrepreneurs dug a mine near Cerralvo and not so far from Platita to extract silver is another of several remarkable instances of convergence.

Consistent with a decision at Calabaza to make the longer journey across the continent to the west and to move along without delay, Cabeza de Vaca suggests they were frustrated in trying to go down the road at a steady pace from village to village. Prior to arriving at Calabaza, when they thought they were getting near Pánuco, some 315 to 325 miles further away, they were content to stay two weeks in Cincuenta. After the visit at Calabaza, they rarely spent more than two nights at any one village and typically stayed only one

For about eighty miles from the vicinity of Ciudad Mier, the Cerralvo Trail followed upstream the Río El Alamo and its tributary creeks and then passed from creek to creek through the site of Cerralvo and down to Platita near Los Ramones.[321] Upon departing Calabaza, the Europeans began to see ahead a mountain range, the Sierra Los Picachos, as they turned to the southwest and up the Río Los Magueyes.[322] Along the path, "all the people" of Calabaza, wrote Cabeza de Vaca, "went with us" to Zapatos, the village of shoes or moccasins. After the ministry to the sick, the four were fed roasted venison from a deer that had been killed that day.[323]

The four bearded males, dressed in only a few pieces of leather, were trying to walk through the country to the next village down a trail near the forested mountains. Hundreds, possibly thousands of native people, men, women, and children, were pushing their way to get close, begging one or another to touch them, to stop and pray for them, to bless their children, and to heal their sick. The four *curadores* were trying both to accommodate the many requests and to move along the trail to the next village. However, they were "hindered" by repeated stops as the people pressed in. "All along this trail," Cabeza de Vaca recorded, "we had great difficulty with the many people who followed us, and we could not get away from them, although we tried because their pressure in coming up to touch us was very great."[324]

At Curados, the village of many cures, about four and a half miles farther southwest from Zapatos, there was another all-night celebration with "songs and dances" after the villagers witnessed the rites and prayers. Here the *físicos* were offered the powder of ground mesquite beans and many ripe tunas as it was now early July.[325] From Curados, they walked about eighteen miles to Ciegos, just north of the town of Hidalgo, the village of those who were blind in one eye.[326] There they crossed several mountain creeks in succession as they were led about fifteen more miles to Platita in the vicinity of the small town of Los Ramones.[327]

On the way to Ciegos and Platita, they could see some sierras other than those nearby. "Here we began to see mountains, and it seemed that they came unbroken from the North Sea," Cabeza de Vaca wrote. He indicated that he was impressed with their great size and beauty.[328] These were the peaks of the Sierra Madre Oriental.[329] A southbound traveler could walk to the base of those sierras and turn east, left, to go to the shore of the Gulf of Mexico. Congruent with what the local people told the Spaniards, the slopes of (still another line of mountains) the Sierra de San Carlos, (south of Burgos), with some peaks about 3,500 feet high, rise within about forty-five miles of the sea.[330]

By this time, Cabeza de Vaca had learned he could depend on Esteban the Black, who had impressive gifts in communication. Originally from sub-Saharan Africa but sold into slavery on the west coast of Morocco, he probably spoke Arabic and Portuguese, which were widely used there.[331] On this journey, he was not relegated to the limitations of a mere domestic slave; rather he was trusted with authority to deal with the people of each village. In effect, he became the spokesman for the four.[332]

Upon departing Platita, they mounted the Bustamante Trail that cut to the west and around the southern tip of the Sierra de Papagayos. Since this path eventually turned almost due north toward Garza Ayala and crossed the upper reaches of tributaries of the Río El Alamo, it could have been met by simply continuing west from Calabaza. Why then did they take the long way around?

The explanation may lie in the custom of the raids that began on this leg of the journey. Those who escorted the four to the next village would, upon arrival with the European *físicos*, pilfer bows, arrows, deerskins, arrowheads, clay pots, and other items of personal property. "They took from them what they had," much to the chagrin of Cabeza de Vaca, "and would even go by the dwellings [or huts] and steal whatever they found."[333] Since the village received advance word that they were coming, they expected this criminal act, hid some of their things, and were eager to recoup their losses by committing the same theft against the next village.

If the people at Calabaza were anything like those at Platita, who plundered their neighbor villages, they would have deliberately misled the Spaniards with half-truths and lies. They may have had enemies further upstream the Río El Alamo and did not wish them to receive the healings and blessings. Instead of pointing them due west, they sent the four southwest to the villages of Zapatos and Curados thereby forcing them through the site of Cerralvo.

104

Based on a sworn statement given to Alonso De León by an indigenous man in 1643, exactly "108 years before," or in 1535, after the "good man," Cabeza de Vaca, traveled through the region, having "preached goodness," he "disappeared marching to the west."[334] To make this maneuver—inland and to the west from Platita near Los Ramones—the *físicos* had to resist pressure from the people of Platita.

Because the local men cajoled them to go south instead of west on the Bustamante Trail, the Spaniards stayed another night. Two Platita scouts were sent ostensibly to check the route; they returned to report that it was a bad path without prickly pears, and the four would have to go "very far" to find people and food.[335]

While some of the Platita women waited nearby to carry their things, Cabeza de Vaca responded to each petition with the equivalent of "sorry, but no." Finally, the Platita women were told to drop the deerskin shoulder bags full of food, skins, and other gifts, leaving the four to travel alone and carry their own loads.

It was probably best for the four *físicos* that they did not know how far and how difficult would be the path they had chosen. To cross the continent to the Pacific coast, they would have to climb mountains, sweat through deserts, hike between the flanks of large canyons, go through valleys, meander through forests, and wade across that same large river. From this point near Platita, they would have to depart alone and carry their own loads. No guides went with them. Crucially, they had lost the highly favored status and esteem first bestowed on them at Cincuenta. What would happen next?

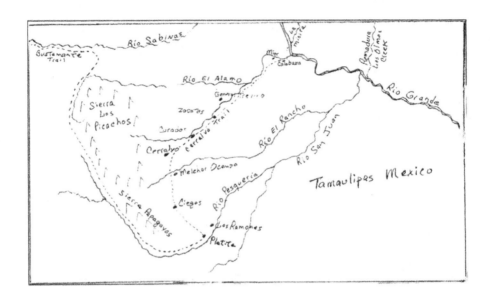

Map 11- THE CERRALVO TRAIL. From the village of Calabaza, they followed the Cerralvo Trail about 80 miles so as to pass "from the north" near the site of the town of Cerralvo and parallel to the mountains, the Picachos and the Papagayos, to Platita, the village at which they turned west or "inland."

Chapter 10
Over the Sierra de La Gloria

The four Spaniards stuffed their food, deerskin blankets, and other belongings into bundles and were ready to march west alone upstream the Río Pesqueria. This creek flowed through the grassy "plain" that spread out between the nearby Sierra Papagayos to their right, when they were facing due west, and the higher Sierra Madre Oriental in the distance that stood both straight ahead and also to their left.

The Platita elders promised that many more gifts, such as flint knives and baskets of ripe sweet tunas, would be forthcoming if the four travelers turned to wade across the creek and continue south to the base of the distant sierras. Although this was the path to Pánuco, the Spaniards wanted to avoid the bad people who, so they had been told, lived down that way. The four travelers did not keep most of the gifts anyway; instead, they offered them to their guides from the last village.[336] They were more interested in making headway on the trail to New Spain while avoiding any groups that practiced violence or slavery. We "did not want to do" what they asked, Cabeza de Vaca recorded, and when "they saw our will, with much sorrow [they] took leave of us and returned down river to their homes."[337]

Without runners sent ahead or guides at their side, the four Europeans set out carrying their own loads. Somewhere ahead, broadly to the west, was the South Sea. This they knew. How far was it? This they did not know. How far north did other Europeans live along the Pacific coast? They had no idea. What obstacles lay before them on the way? They were blissfully unaware. However, their leader believed if they just kept marching, eventually they would find their goal.

At sunset, after another long all-day hike that left them exhausted, they arrived at a small community and treated the sick. The people of this village, although they had heard about the four strangers, knew nothing of the spirit of Cincuenta. The four were not heralded as before. It seemed the *físicos* had lost the highly favored status along with the celebrations and the pampering that had followed them from Cincuenta in Texas, on the other side of the great river.

The next morning as they were preparing to embark, the Platita men, whom Cabeza de Vaca did not highly esteem, suddenly appeared. Having changed their mind and walked through the night, they summarily stole whatever they found along the way. They had pestered and annoyed the Spaniards, but they reinstated the high standing that had been lost. The bearded ones are "children of the sun," they announced. Great power is in their hands to cure the sick or to kill their hosts if they did not offer them ample food and all their possessions. They must tell those in the next village to favor them in the same way.[338]

The four children of the sun began a long travel segment of several hundred miles on a zigzag route to the north by northwest back into Texas.[339] In the late summer heat, they were making a sort of loop around the worst of the desert, although they didn't know it. Their route was determined by a thin line of fresh water that depended on the few extra showers of rain that typically fall in August and September, especially in the mountains of Coahuila. To Cabeza de Vaca, it appeared to be "a great detour" that he disliked. He "always considered it certain that going toward the sunset," and not so far to the north, they "would find" other Europeans.[340] In his mind, the continent was not so wide, and he probably thought they were not far from that part of New Spain that he knew was on the west coast.

Without knowledge of the land and the people, they had to follow their guides. If directed to the north, they assumed it was the proper route to coastal lands to the west. They were not leisurely going about to visit this place or that.[341] Their desire to explore unknown lands was secondary to that of finding New Spain. They were attempting to traverse "the whole land," or to cross the entire continent, so that from the shores of "the South Sea," the Pacific, they could go home to the European world from which they had come.[342]

The other three were now in agreement with the decisions of Cabeza de Vaca. Under his leadership, upon arriving at each indigenous settlement, the Spaniards unfolded a unique *modus operandi,* the main act of which was their work for the infirm. Everything was predicated on the desire to keep moving along the trails, one day at a time, one village at a time. Using sign language, Esteban consulted with local leaders, then reported what he had learned.[343] Four messengers were chosen, one for each of them, to run ahead and notify the next settlement they were on the way. They asked for a few guides to walk with them, although at times there was a train of hundreds or thousands. The message about the four *físicos* shot down the trails at lightning speed, and when they arrived, the people already knew who they were.[344]

From Platita near Los Ramones, they made their way to Cascabel, the village of the copper rattle, and then to Río Hermoso, the village in which Cabeza de Vaca performed surgery on a dying man. At these two villages, the Spaniards began to connect with the Aztec empire of the recent past and with the future expeditions of Marcos de Niza (1539) and Francisco de Coronado (1540-42), both of whom they themselves unwittingly stimulated.

Cascabel sat on the near side of a mountain and Río Hermoso on the banks of a "lovely river" on the other side of the same sierra. The path between included a segment of some twenty-one miles, or seven leagues, up in the heights.[345] Along this mountain pass, Cabeza de Vaca noticed what appeared to be rocks of iron ore, and somewhere nearby were herds of bison and pine trees with many tasty pine nuts that were offered to them. All these indicators are found in and around the Sierra de La Gloria, a mountain range with some peaks over 6,000 feet, that extends about thirty-seven miles to the southeast from the city of Monclova, Coahuila.

To arrive at Cascabel at the foot of the Sierra de La Gloria, following the Bustamante Trail, the four walked west from Platita and then to the northwest along the Río Pesqueria and its tributaries.[346] With the Sierra Milpillas to their left, they hiked over the divide and followed another mountain creek that turned from flowing west to a course that was "straight to the north," along about the same geographic angle as Mexican Highway 85.[347] After a visit at a large village of friendly people near Garza Ayala, they turned upstream the Río Sabinas further "inland … more than" 150 miles, or fifty leagues.[348]

Both narratives mention mountain "skirts," *haldas*, or "flanks" near which they walked.[349] This was a reference to the spectacular slopes seen on either side of the *Cañon de Sabinas* and the *Cañon de Bustamante* as the men went through the sites of the towns of Sabinas Hidalgo, Villaldama, Bustamante, and Soledad de Abajo. Beyond the two canyons, they followed a creek that runs down from the west side of the Sierra de La Gloria and joins the Río El Salado, a tributary of the Río Sabinas.[350] They hiked alongside this creek through a semi-arid shrub land or desert plain that appeared to stretch out forever in the distance.

Still walking barefoot, possibly with more bleeding wounds, through this flat plateau, they gradually approached the west side of the main line of the Sierra de La Gloria.[351] There, "at the foot of the mountains," sat the village of Cascabel.[352] "Paper-shell piñon pines" with "characteristics that match remarkably well the description given by Cabeza de Vaca," have been observed in these sierras.[353] Researchers have also collected "rocks resembling iron slag" in these same "mountains south and southeast of Monclova."[354]

From Cascabel, the four Spaniards "entered the mountains." They must have broken into a sweat as they climbed up into the higher elevation of about 4,000 feet to walk over the divide. After traversing the mountain pass of twenty-one miles, they descended to Río Hermoso. This village sat on a creek that flows west from the higher peaks to the east and then turns north to go through the town of Castaños where it is called the Río Bocatoche.[355] In a region that is mostly rocky and barren, this riverside venue presented a beautiful, *hermoso*, view of a rushing mountain stream. Cabeza de Vaca mentions gifts of bison hides at Río Hermoso, which suggests that the site was within hunting range of the herds.[356] In fact, many credible bison sightings were reported in Chihuahua, Coahuila, and Nuevo Leon from the 1500s to well into the 1800s. One herd was living in northwestern Chihuahua in the 1990s.[357]

With the twists and turns of the river, the total distance, between Platita near Los Ramones and Cascabel on the west side of the Sierra de La Gloria, is 240 to 260 miles, which harmonizes with the narrative estimates. A rough measure of the distance along this route from Los Rios Tres, at the mouth of Ygnacio Creek on the Nueces River (of 135 miles to Calabaza and 80 miles more to Platita, plus 240 to 250 miles to Cascabel) also fits reasonably well with the 450 miles, 150 leagues, referenced in *Historia General*.[358] Now in late August or early September, Cabeza de Vaca and his companions, when they passed through this region of the Sierra de La Gloria, entered the cultural sphere of pre-Colonial Mexico. The Mexica-Aztec coalition of cities that ruled the Valley of Mexico from about 1428 to 1521 had connections far and wide. Built high in the sierras yet on a cluster of islands in a big lake, Tenochtitlán dazzled Cortés and the other *conquistadores* when they arrived in 1519. The famous metropolis was in place as late as the spring of 1521, only six years before Cabeza de Vaca left Spain on the

Narváez expedition. When the four Spaniards made this long trek in 1535, the indigenous people in these distant communities had not heard about the conquest and the destruction of the city. Tenochtitlán was still standing, they falsely assumed, and still under the rule of the Aztecs.

Every day at the summits of pyramid temples, cruel Aztec priests ripped out the hearts of their prisoners, including children. Nonetheless, the Aztecs achieved a uniquely advanced civilization that included the erection of some tall structures such as the great Templo Mayor. At about 200 feet, it was higher than a twelve-story building. The Aztecs made impressive achievements in agriculture, craftsmanship, commerce, trade, art, architecture, calendars, music, dance, and poetry.[359] In Tenochtitlán, there were busy markets with an abundance of food and other things they valued, including cotton blankets, tools, jewelry, and molten-metal, decorative objects such as copper rattles or bells, which the Spaniards called *cascabels*.[360] The Aztecs also traded for bison hides, cacao (chocolate) beans, colorful bird feathers, and "great pieces of jade" that, because they were "translucent green," appeared to be emeralds.[361]

In the early 1500s, traders and carriers on the way from Cascabel in the Sierra de La Gloria to Tenochtitlán and the Valley of Mexico traversed an interior route that ran from there north by northwest. Used before the arrival of the Spanish *conquistadores* with their horses, this network of roads was taken somewhat unhappily by Cabeza de Vaca and his companions. A barrier to a direct southbound route to Tenochtitlán from the area of the Sierra de La Gloria was formed by the high mountains of the Sierra Madre Oriental and by hostile Chichimecas and other indigenous groups.

While Cabeza de Vaca had heard about the wonderful accomplishments of the Aztecs, he and his group had seen only a primitive level of development among the people of Florida, Texas, Tamaulipus, and Nuevo Leon. Some of them made excellent bows, arrows, fish nets, flint knives, clay pots, and spears. However, none of the indigenous people of those regions were metalwork craftsmen who made useful and artistic products out of molten metal such as copper or silver. The four physicians certainly were stricken with wonder when they saw a little gift tendered at Cascabel at the foot of the mountains of the Sierra de La Gloria.

A group of donors, who were travelers and not the residents, handed Dorantes, after his services for the sick, some cotton blankets and a copper *cascabel*. Several inches long with the form of a human face indented on the side, it was a handsome, molten-metal object made by an artisan who had carefully prepared a mold. The intriguing object had been made, or offered in trade, so the Spaniards were informed, by a great nation that was far away.[362] There were miners who dug ore and craftsmen who smelted metals and worked with molds.[363] More *cascabels,* cotton blankets, and other things were available there.[364] From what the indigenous people indicated by their hand signs, the Spaniards surmised that the distant nation sat near, or on the shore of, a sea, which they thought was the South Sea (Pacific Ocean).[365]

The standard route to the distant nation of many *cascabels* began "toward the north" from the Sierra de La Gloria. In an honest response to the Spaniards' inquiry, the indigenous people directed them to the road, the La Boquilla Trail, that would lead to the prosperous city. For the residents of the villages in the Sierra de La Gloria and for other Amerindians of that age, the location of a distant place was indicated by pointing to the path that took you there, in this case "toward the north."

After Cabeza de Vaca and the others arrived at the village on a lovely river, they showed the people there the ornamental copper rattle. Those of Río Hermoso were well acquainted with such objects and with those who had given it to Dorantes. The traveler-donor group must have passed through Río Hermoso just a day or two before meeting the Spaniards. Coming down the same road from opposite directions, the two groups met at Cascabel. On their way home from a trading mission, the donors gave misleading comments about the valuable items in their loads perhaps to avoid being subjected to theft and physical harm.[366] Those of Río Hermoso also spoke glowingly of the distant nation where one could trade for *cascabels* and cotton blankets. They described a community that was "richer," or *mas rica*, that sat on a sea and had permanent houses.

When at Cascabel, the local people lifted arm and hand to point broadly to the north to the trail that would lead there; the Spaniards mistakenly understood them to be indicating that the wealthy nation was actually "to the north" from there. In truth, the mysterious nation with permanent houses was to the south. The standard road, which made a zig-zag route to the north approximately 450 miles, was the same set of trails the Spaniards were now following. Near Pecos, Texas, the path cut back to the south to follow Toyah Creek, the Rio Grande, the Río Conchos, the Río Florido, the Río Parral, and other rivers until it eventually ascended to Tenochtitlán in the Valley of Mexico.

These donors, whom the four met at Cascabel, may have been traders who had gone along these same trails to the Pecos River to follow it upstream into New Mexico, where the Pueblo people, for decades, had carried on trade with merchants from Tenochtitlán. The Pueblos kept valuables that came from the Aztecs, including copper rattles and cotton blankets. The traveling band the Spaniards met at Cascabel obtained some of these products that had been offered in Tenochtitlán or another of the Aztec-related cities in the Valley of Mexico.

The four Europeans misunderstood these descriptions to be a reference to a site on the Pacific coast, or the South Sea. However, the donors were referring to the fact that the great city of Tenochtitlán had been built on a cluster of islands in an inland sea. More Aztec-related cities sat on the edge of this large lake that was surrounded by mountains. Visitors from the north had the impression that it was a sea, as described to Cabeza de Vaca and his companions.[367]

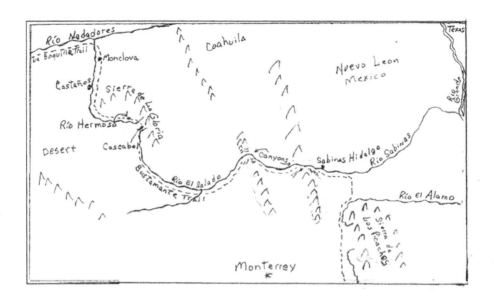

Map 12- THE BUSTAMANTE TRAIL. For about 250 miles from
Platita, near the southern tip of the Papagayos mountains, the four
followed the Bustamante Trail upstream the Rio Pesqueria and west
on the Rio Sabinas and the Rio El Salado until they turned north to
Cascabel, the village at the base of the Sierra de la Gloria where
they first heard about the richer nation "to the north."

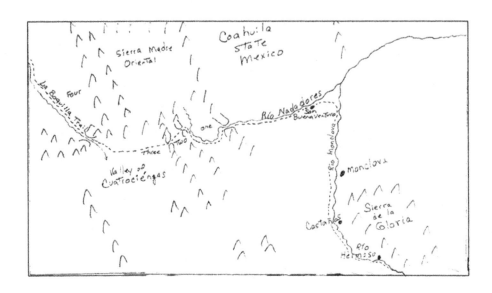

Map 13- THE LA BOQUILLA TRAIL. From Rio Hermoso on
the La Boquilla Trail, the four traveled north then turned west
through four valleys, each with a narrow canyon entrance. The first
was the Valley of Lamadrid through which flows the Rio
Nadadores. Valley three was Cuatrociénegas and four was Calaveras
where they began marching "to the north" for "many days"
through uninhabited regions.

Chapter 11
Back to the Rio Grande

The night the four arrived at Río Hermoso, the village at a lovely river, some of the local people brought a seriously injured man to the four *físicos*. They explained that "long ago" he had been shot in his right shoulder and the arrow point lodged deep within his chest. No one had been able to get it out. In great pain, the man was always sick and surely near death.

Due to his fear of failure, Castillo, the son of a physician in Spain, never would have attempted a hard case like this. The year before at Los Ríos Dos on the Nueces River, he had refused to take as his patient a dying man in a nearby camp. Dorantes, who did just enough to keep the four Europeans on the trail to New Spain, would not have devoted the required time and effort to serve a native person. Cabeza de Vaca, on the other hand, expressed a genuine concern for the indigenous people and crafted an argument for their humane treatment. Instead of making them slaves and stealing their property, we should, he wrote, "cherish" the native people "as brothers."[368] It fell on him to be a compassionate doctor and nurse to this poor man.

Cabeza de Vaca always began with a prayer for a cure. Since the travelers arrived at night and left the next morning, he must have arranged for the man to lie down on some animal skins in a well-lit place near a bonfire. Getting down on his knees, the surgeon pulled out his flint knife and began. It may have taken an hour or more to make an incision that was large enough. Many eyes gathered around to watch as he struggled through a bloody mess. At times, it appeared the arrow point had won the battle. Finally, he was able to pull it out. Then he made two stitches and stanched the bleeding with scrapings of fat from a bison hide. In the morning before they departed, he took out the stitches and the man said that "he felt no pain or hurt at all." The people carried the arrow point far and wide to show and tell.[369]

Even though the operation took place in Coahuila, Mexico, Cabeza de Vaca may legitimately be named, as he has been, the first Texas surgeon and the patron saint of the Texas Surgical Society.[370] During the previous five years in Texas, he had served as a *físico* and, consistent with a more conventional practice of medicine, had performed surgeries and cauterizations when appropriate.

If the esteem, which had been taken by word of mouth from place to place, was about to decline into a less intensive form, it was renewed afresh when the people saw the individual attention he gave to this desperate man and to others.[371] After such sterling success, the four were so highly regarded that many of the local people, at times "three or four thousand," wanted to walk with them to the next village. Clearly, it was mainly Cabeza de Vaca who merited praise, but all four were deemed worthy.

A few days after leaving Río Hermoso, which was nestled near the base of the mountains, probably twelve-to-fifteen miles southeast of Castaños, as they were on the way to another village, Cabeza de Vaca noticed some of their guides were preparing for a hunt. The local men, each brandishing a two-foot stick, lined up to walk arm-to-arm through an area that was thickly covered with tall grasses. When a large rabbit jumped up, those nearest quickly struck it or grabbed it. Their way of making the chase was "a marvelous thing" to see, he wrote, and "when we halted at night … each of us" had "eight or ten … of them."[372]

The story of the rabbit hunt as they were passing through one of "those valleys" contains enough evidence to locate this venue.

118

However, the clues about the next series of travel segments are few from this point, and, at times, vague or misleading. Cabeza de Vaca tells us that his aim was to write an account that was "brief rather than lengthy" and that he could not recall many things.[373] *Historia General*, the other narrative, does not supply us with much information about the rest of the route either.[374]

After the rabbit hunt, the four *físicos* passed through a series of valleys and walked "many days …without meeting any other people," in part alongside some sierras in which there were deer and other wild game.[375] Following the La Boquilla Trail through dry, "uninhabited" lands, they forded a substantial body of water that was flowing broadly "from the north." Then they marched about ninety miles over several days to a mysterious grassy plain where they met a large group from several bands coming to meet them.

From Río Hermoso at the base of the Sierra de La Gloria, the four followed the La Boquilla Trail alongside a creek, the Río Bocatoche, to the site of Castaños and on to the north where it poured into the Río Monclova. Passing directly through the site of the city of Monclova, they continued north toward the confluence with the Río Nadadores near the site of San Buenaventura. Cabeza de Vaca's use of the plural form "valleys" harmonizes with the fact that westbound, beginning with a travel segment upstream the Río Nadadores, there are four topographical depressions, or basins, in succession, between mountains, each with a narrow canyon entrance from the east.[376]

Along the upstream path of the Río Nadadores, the four *físicos* traveled west into the first valley, known as La Madrid. At the valley entrance, there is a canyon with steep walls called the Cariño de la Montaña. In the canyon floor on both river banks, desert cottontail rabbits hid among thick stands of tall, succulent grasses that still grow there.[377]

Leaving behind the Nadadores, whose upstream path turns north out of the Valley of La Madrid into the Sierra del Cristo, the four Spaniards continued westbound through two mountain passes and a small second valley in between and entered the third, the Valley of Cuatrociénegas. This was an important travel stop because it was the final habitable place with plenty of fresh water at the edge of the inhospitable desert to the north and west. The basin of Cuatrociénegas has its own ecosystem with several springs, pools, a short river, and four marshy areas thickly covered with grasses and weeds.

A multitude now accompanied them, not only through the valleys over to the region of Cuatrociénegas, but also on the long stretch through the desert up to the great river and still farther north back into the United States. They turned north because to the west lay the arid Bolsón de Mapimí which was part of a large barren desert. From southern New Mexico to the northern border of Zacatecas, the Chihuahuan Desert was an enormous barrier to travel by foot. The bison herds could find grassy fields and water at springs, arroyos, and even lakes that filled once a year; but the lifeless desert was hostile to mortal men.

The route to the ford on the Rio Grande began with a walk through the canyon to the north of the Valley of Cuatrociénegas. Well before 1535, native traders had discovered this natural pass through a split in the sierras that fringed the northern rim of the basin and through which ran a small creek. From here, they made a long loop to the north and passed over two fords, not of different rivers, as Cabeza de Vaca thought, but of a single "large river flowing from the north," the Rio Grande.

Despite all the obstacles that Cabeza de Vaca and the others confronted on this journey, things seemed to fall into place for them. Had they attempted to walk this leg of the journey, from Cuatrociénegas to the southern tip of the Big Bend and north into Texas any other time of year, they may have died of thirst. Through Coahuila, they followed a small intermittent stream, fed by late summer mountain showers. The creek flowed down from the

120

heights through the fourth valley or depression, the Valle de Las Calaveras.[378]

As they trekked near the foot of a line of small mountains, their guides climbed up into the higher meadows, traveling parallel to the path below. Up in the heights they killed deer and later brought them down to the four heroes. On this part of the journey, there was plenty of food. It was now August or September 1535, and, at about 4,000 feet, the air was warm but not so hot as they began to descend into the watershed of the Rio Grande.[379] Following northbound to the great river, their guides were helping them circumnavigate the worst of the desert.

Just to the west of the mouth of the Río La Boquilla, a small creek that flows north to the southernmost tip of the Big Bend, there is a sharp curve in the Rio Grande so that, at that riparian segment, the flow is indeed "from the north." It is unlikely this crossing, the second, could have been downstream from this point since the terrain is too rugged, and the flow through there is not from the north but from the south or southwest. The Río Alamos, or Babía, which they would have crossed on the proposed Nueva Rosita route, flows from the northwest to be sure, but it could not be described as "large."[380]

Had there been from the Valley of Cuatrociénegas, Coahuila, through which they passed, a major native trail straight across the desert to the site of Ciudad Camargo on the Río Conchos, it would have been a trek of some 220 miles. However, in 1535, the native people who lived there had no horses, and there was no major trail through that section of the Chihuahuan Desert. The actual route they took, with its detour deep into Trans Pecos Texas, and then down to the area near the mouth of the Río Florido, was closer to 770 miles, or more than three times as far.

The Nueva Rosita route, to the east downstream the Nadadores before turning northwest upstream along the Sabinas and the Babia, is a dubious proposal.[381] If the four arrived at the Rio Grande after going through some "valleys" and after "many days" (perhaps twelve to fourteen) alongside mountain ranges in uninhabited country, as the narrative says, this rules out the Nueva Rosita proposal. On it, they would not have passed through any valleys or beside any mountain ranges for at least the first 150 miles from Río Hermoso, south of Castaños. Also, on the Nueva Rosita route they would have, contrary to the record, passed thorough inhabited areas with native villages along the rivers.

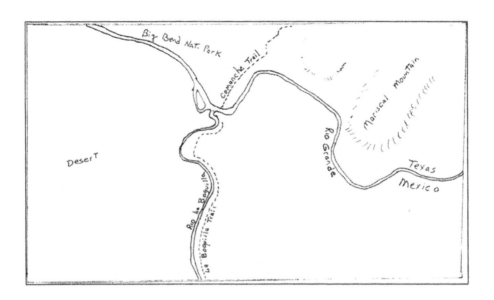

Map 14- THE SECOND CROSSING OF THE RIO GRANDE.
Heading north, they crossed back into the United States at the
mouth of the Rio La Boquilla where, due to its configuration at that
site, the great river appeared to be "coming from the north."

Chapter 12
The Long Trek Deep into Texas

Álvar Cabeza de Vaca and his group departed the Valley of Cuatrociénegas with hundreds of indigenous people following, and hiked "many days," in part along the base of several lines of desert mountains. The four Spaniards presented themselves as confident travelers who had somehow gotten lost but now wanted to go to the South Sea, the Pacific coastal region. The message that they were coming was carried speedily down the trails by four runners who were sent ahead. Admired by the local people at each village, many wanted to go with them as they marched deeper into these unknown lands. Row after row of brown men, women, and children walked with the four grizzly, bearded men and carried their packs and blankets over their shoulders; they occasionally stopped to drink from a stream.

Among the inhabitants of the Far Away Lands of northern Mexico and far west Texas, the four Europeans, in this year of 1535, rapidly had become celebrities with a reputation for many cures. Under the leadership of the compassionate Cabeza de Vaca, they offered as a traveler's gift their service as *curadores,* healers, or *físicos,* physicians. Since this was a social office with which the people were familiar, the Spaniards could not have chosen a better identity to obtain favorable treatment. Already, the indigenous people had *físicos* who, except for the prayers and the sign of the cross, employed similar remedies and techniques. They responded warmly to the four Europeans and eagerly brought their sick and injured to them.

Desperately trying to find their way to the Spanish conquerors on the west coast, Cabeza de Vaca and his three companions did not know how far it was and neither did they know the correct path to get there. Passing through Coahuila and Trans Pecos, Texas, between the Pecos River and the Rio Grande, they preferred to go west, but the local people were telling them that there was no water, or food, or people that way. Following their guides, they kept going north.

Cabeza de Vaca used such phrases as "far away" or "extremely far away" to describe their travel through this region. It appears that he and the other bearded ones were astounded at the scale of everything around them. The distances were far. The land and the desert, wide. The mountains, high. The water of the great river, abundant. And the number of people who wanted to be with them, enormous.

Although they rested each night in a camp or village, the day trips were sometimes very tiring. A few years later, in Spain, Cabeza de Vaca was still feeling the exhaustion. Along with the other three, he survived this epic journey because he knew that in the face of weariness, deprivations, and obstacles, they must press ahead with resilience on the trail to New Spain.

To paraphrase what Cabeza de Vaca wrote: "We learned that we could walk all day without eating until night. At times, we had only a little food. Our guides were astonished at how well we endured the difficulties of the journey; we never seemed to be too tired to keep going. We were accustomed to hardships, and we paid no attention to fatigue, nor did we let it hinder us."[382]

The four assiduously avoided revealing to their Native American patrons that they were members of the brutal tribe who some years earlier had defeated the Aztecs in the Valley of Mexico. During and after the war horrible atrocities had been committed, including torture, murder, rape, and slavery. The native people might turn against them if they perceived a connection with the Spanish, but they appeared to know nothing at all about the conquest.

Those who later in the march accompanied Cabeza de Vaca and his group to the region near Culiacán were confounded when told that the traveling healers were of the same tribe as the Spanish *conquistadores*. The latter were arresting them to sell as slaves and were hated and feared for their avarice and cruelty. The way the indigenous people made a distinction between them may be paraphrased and amplified in this way:

"The four travelers came from where the sun rises, whereas the *conquistadores* came from where the sun sets. The four healers cured the sick, whereas the *conquistadores* killed the healthy. The four peacemakers came unarmed, barefoot, and almost naked as we are; but the *conquistadores* were fully clothed; they rode horses and carried lances and swords. The four servants were not greedy for anything; indeed, they handed their gifts to others and kept nothing, whereas the *conquistadores* stole everything they found and offered no gifts to anyone. In sum, the deeds of the four were praiseworthy while those of the *conquistadores* were violent and caused suffering and death. Therefore, the four físicos cannot be of the same tribe as the *conquistadores*."[383]

At the southernmost segment of the Big Bend, the travelers arrived at the waters of a *gran río* that flowed "from the north." They saw the banks were lined with green brush and trees that contrasted sharply with the browns, grays, and reds of the surrounding desert. The four did not, as some books mistakenly say, attempt to walk northwest from there alongside the river.[384] About twenty-five miles upstream, they would have been blocked by the steep walls of the Santa Elena Canyon, a marvel of nature with sheer limestone cliffs that rise over 1,500 feet from the desert floor.[385]

Instead of traveling *alongside* the Rio Grande upstream to the northwest, Cabeza de Vaca and the other *físicos* crossed and then walked *away from* it.[386] Following one of the Comanche Trails that meandered north from the river, they were the first outsiders to witness the famous sunrises, sunsets, and night sky of Big Bend National Park.[387] To their west, they saw the Chisos Mountains with several peaks that rise into the sky to an elevation of more than 7,000 feet. Within one day of hiking, they could have reached the southeast-flowing Tornillo Creek to follow upstream Maravillas Creek and Pena Colorado Creek.[388]

Cabeza de Vaca recorded that upon fording the great river, they walked over "some plains of ninety miles."[389] Since it is rugged and mountainous for miles around, his words cannot mean that the plains were near the river, for there are none. He was not, as some have thought, writing "fairy tales" or "exaggerations and fictions" to increase "sales."[390] On the other hand, although he is trying to tell his readers what really happened, at times he used inexact language, and, at a few places, his memory failed him.

The "plains" are not ninety miles in length, and not, as he seems to say, adjacent to the great river; rather, they begin at the point of the town of Marathon, Texas, which is about that distance to the north. Approximately thirty miles in length and up to ten miles wide, this plain lies partly between the Glass Mountains and the Woods Hollow Mountains. It is an area of wide-open spaces, which reminded an early settler of the plains of Marathon in Greece, and through which flows an intermittent stream. Geologists have discovered that the green Marathon Plains sit atop a broad, domal uplift of bedrock with an overlay of alluvial dirt that supports short, sparse grasses as well as cacti, yucca, creosote bushes, and cat-claw.[391]

As the four Europeans and their many admirers hiked through these plains of Marathon, on the horizon ahead, they saw a throng approaching from the opposite direction. It was not a herd of bison but a crowd of people coming to meet the four physician-celebrities. "From far away," Cabeza de Vaca later wrote, "many people came looking for us."[392] Some of them were from the next line of five villages, but others were from another place "extremely far away." There are good reasons to believe those of the latter group were the Coronado Querechos who were encountered a few years later by *conquistadores* in the west Texas plains.

If we can ascertain where the soldiers of Francisco Vázquez de Coronado (1510-1554) were when they met native Americans who had seen Cabeza de Vaca, that could aid in discerning the route through these lands. Coronado was appointed to search for a great, wealthy city of gold with very tall houses, because Cabeza de Vaca and his party reported that at several places along their route, such a place was vividly described. The native people pointed to the north, roughly toward New Mexico, to indicate where the rich city was located. Coronado gathered his army in 1540 and explored New Mexico and Arizona. However, he did not find anything even remotely resembling a large, wealthy city with molten metal objects of copper, gold, or silver, and very tall buildings.

Cabeza de Vaca and his three companions did not intentionally mislead anyone about the rich city "to the north." Prior to 1521, there was indeed a large wealthy city in Mexico with gold, silver, and tall buildings. It was the Aztec metropolis of Tenochtitlán in the Valley of Mexico to the south. It had been destroyed by Cortez, and on its ruins, Mexico City was built. From each place that they were told about this great city, the trail to arrive there started out "to the north" before turning to the south along the Río Florido and the Río Parral. News traveled slowly in the 1500s. In 1535, the indigenous people of northern Mexico thought the great city was still there; they had not heard about its destruction.

In the spring of 1541, still looking for the rich city, now called "Quivira," Coronado's army left the Pueblo villages along the Rio Grande and set out to the east.[393] From the Pecos River in the area of Fort Sumner, they meandered, following streams, first to the northeast and then turned southeast to enter Blanco Canyon south of Floydada, Texas, where artifacts of the Spanish campsite have been found.[394] They lived here for a while with a band of Querechos, who fondly remembered Cabeza de Vaca and his party.

128

The Querechos had seen the four not at Blanco Canyon but at another site "toward New Spain" or further south.[395]

With this information, we can put together what happened. In the fall of 1535, one of the four messengers sent by the Cabeza de Vaca party arrived at a Querecho camp, somewhere in the west Texas plains, to announce that the four famous physicians were soon to pass through. Many of the people went down to meet them at the Marathon Plains. The Querechos then turned back to make several overnight, one-day trips with the Europeans along the right bank of the Pecos River. In a few days, they all arrived at Recepción on Toyah Creek, the first of five "clusters" of villages.[396] A Querecho woman who traveled with them later gave birth to a baby girl with white skin, a child of one of the white Europeans.[397]

The Querechos offered Coronado's men a large stack of bison blankets expecting that they would give them back to others as Cabeza de Vaca had done at Recepción. Also, they wanted Coronado's men to touch them and pray for them in the manner of Cabeza de Vaca. But the avaricious soldiers of Coronado kept all the hides and were not interested in offering any blessing or prayer.[398] This left the poor Querechos bewildered, and they were not inclined to help Coronado.

To confirm the location of Recepción and the other well-populated villages, we are aided by the records of two missionary expeditions of the early 1580s. From reading *Los Naufragios*, the narrative penned by Álvar Cabeza de Vaca himself and first published in 1542, Franciscan volunteers were motivated to make long, dangerous journeys to the north from New Spain. The Franciscan priest Agustín Rodríguez (1520?-1582) was so moved by its words that he decided to go to the Far Away Lands with a companion, Friar Francisco López, to attempt to Christianize some of the indigenous people described in the book.

The chronicles of these two expeditions provide a detailed description of the trails taken earlier by Cabeza de Vaca. On the first of two expeditions (1581-82), Rodríguez and his companion were taken north along the Río Conchos, over some mountains, then up the Río Grande to the Pueblo people of New Mexico north of Albuquerque where both were soon killed. On the second journey (1582-83), Antonio Espejo (1540?-1585?) and his party, with his able assistant Diego Pérez de Luxán (1540?-1590?), searched for the two missionaries in the hope they were still alive.

Espejo decided to return by a different route to the ford on the Rio Grande at San Bernardino, about fifteen miles north of the Conchos mouth.[399] While passing through the southeastern corner of New Mexico, he met three Querechos who were traveling on foot because the Native Americans still had no horses. The Native Americans offered to show Espejo the best trails back to the ford. Espejo was then taken to a string of villages on a creek that fed a marshy area with some ponds.

Although they arrived from opposite directions, the geographic route of the Espejo expedition in 1583 converged with that of Cabeza de Vaca in 1535. Some forty-eight years earlier, the four *físicos* also encountered a line of settlements deep in these lands of Trans Pecos, Texas. There is only one place in the region that is near lots of water and trees to support large native villages, and that fits the other descriptive factors. It is Toyah Creek and its feeder stream Madera Creek which flow north to the Pecos River and form a lush oasis in the desert.[400]

To arrive at Recepción and the other Native American villages in this little paradise along Toyah Creek, the Cabeza de Vaca group walked over the plains of Marathon in 1535 to a pass through the Glass Mountains.[401] The group's guides led the four probably to Horsehead Crossing on the Pecos River, not to cross it but, to make an overnight camp near fresh water, trees, and wild game. From here, they traveled forty to fifty miles northwest on the Pecos Trail, along the right bank, to Recepción, the northernmost of five villages on Toyah Creek.

Through flat or gently sloping terrain extending out from the Pecos River, in the wetter age of 1535, these lands were covered in

130

prairie grasses. This corner of the "Great American West" was the edge of the Great Plains that extended north from there into Canada. Álvar Nuñez Cabeza de Vaca and his three traveling companions were the first people of European or African descent to see herds of bison on the prairies of North America. They had previously seen them near San Antonio and in eastern Refugio County, Texas.

The party of Cabeza de Vaca entered the northernmost indigenous settlement, here called Recepción, situated not far from the Toyah Creek mouth on the Pecos River in the fall of 1535. Espejo's expedition entered the same village in the summer of 1583. On both occasions, the Europeans were impressed with the resources and the large number of native people who lived there.[402] This was also the beginning point of the 150-mile Candelaria Trail that led back to the ford on the Rio Grande at San Bernardino.

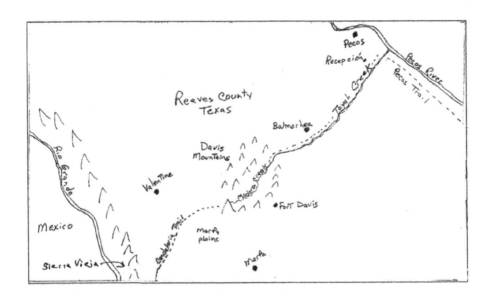

Map 15- THE CANDELARIA TRAIL. After passing through the
Marathon Plains, they met the Pecos River, probably at Horsehead
Crossing, then followed it to the northwest. They turned southwest
alongside Toyah Creek and Madera Creek and over the Marfa
Plains to the Sierra Vieja.

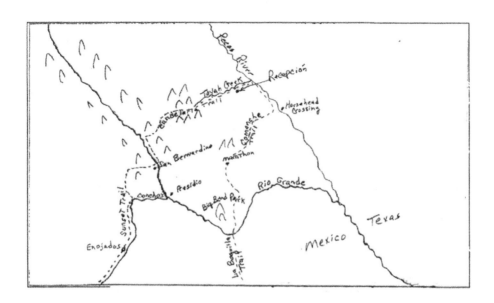

Map 16- DEEP INTO TRANS PECOS TEXAS. After the second crossing of the Rio Grande into Big Bend Park, they followed a branch of the Comanche Trail through the Marathon Plains and turned northwest on the Pecos Trail to the area of the Toyah Creek mouth near Pecos, Texas.

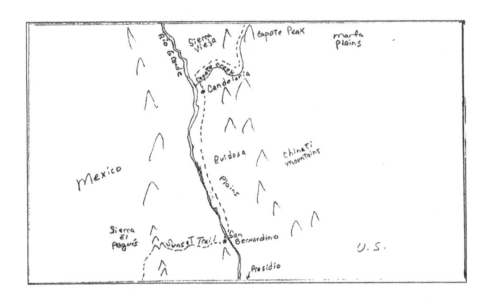

Map 17- THE REGION OF LA JUNTA. The four traveled through the region but did not go to the area of La Junta de Los Rios. Instead, they came down from the north and crossed the great river at San Bernardino, about fifteen miles north of the Conchos mouth. From here, they turned west "toward the setting sun" and went up and over the mountains they saw in the distance, the Sierra El Peguis.

Chapter 13
Through the Davis Mountains

On the trek through the Marathon Plains and on to the north toward the Pecos River, Álvar Cabeza de Vaca must have felt content about their progress on the road to European civilization. As he did not understand why they were still going mostly to the north, while he wanted to go west, they were, from the time of their sojourn at Cincuenta in Texas, treated like celebrities. Beginning at that village, the native people gathered prickly pears and other food and went hunting "solely for ... their benefit."[403] Astounded by this turn of events, he and the other three Spaniards talked among themselves about how if God was now "so good" to them, they should "toil ... somewhat more" both in their service to the people and in pressing forward on the trails.[404]

Their perspective is is summarized in a paraphrase of a few lines from *Historia General*: "Despite the fatigues and inconveniences of so long a road before us, we were determined, even if it took eight years, to keep walking until we found other Europeans. We deemed it a thing of very great wonder that we hiked for months, tended to hundreds of sick patients, and crossed the continent. No one could believe how we did it except those who saw it."[405]

At times they preferred to just eat and rest rather than to say the prayers and make the sign of the cross over their many patients. Nevertheless, they continued their labor of healing as they moved deeper and deeper into Trans Pecos Texas and northern Mexico.

135

While the *físicos* had traveled far, they were beginning to get frustrated because they still had not seen any sign of civilization. They must have questioned why they were still going so far to the north. Soon they faced a series of troubles that cast doubt on their prospects for arrival in New Spain.

The four Spaniards were dependent on their guides to serve as hunters, too, and most evenings on the trail, they roasted fresh meat for them.

"The women carried many mats with which they made dwellings for each of us. . .In the evening when the hunters arrived with the game they had killed, we asked them to roast those deer and hares and everything else they had taken . . . which they did very quickly in some holes they had dug for this purpose. From all of it we took a little and the rest we gave to the leader of the people who had come with us. We told him to divide it among them all. Each one with his allotted share came to us so that we might first bless it by breathing on it, and we made the sign of the cross over it, for otherwise, they would not dare to eat it."[406]

When they arrived at the village of Recepción near the mouth of Toyah Creek, they found the land along its banks was a paradise in the desert where they enjoyed plenty of food and fresh water. There were marshy areas with trees and natural ponds full of fish. Herds of bison were not far away. In the adjacent Davis Mountains, there were pine nuts, berries, and many rabbits, mule deer, and pronghorn antelope. Mesquite trees with edible beans grew along the nearby Pecos River.[407]

A few days after departing Recepción, their guides took the Europeans through a segment of the desert trail that was just the opposite of the lush Toyah Creek. They were led into some "uninhabited land of very rough mountains." It was "so arid" there "was no game in them" and "because of this," Cabeza de Vaca later wrote, "we suffered very great hunger."[408] A bad situation got worse when, in these same dry mountains, many of their guides fell ill, and the caravan came to a halt.[409]

136

The Spaniards could have pushed on alone or, perhaps, with two or three of the native guides who were not ill. In a few days, they would have passed through the dry mountains of affliction to arrive at the next village where there was food and rest. To do this, to abandon their many travel companions who were not well, they would have to ignore the pleadings of the sick. Under the leadership of Cabeza de Vaca, the four *físicos* chose to do the right thing. Their next meal was postponed as they stopped "to bless . . . and breathe upon" the infirm.[410]

As they traveled through Trans Pecos Texas and northern Mexico, the people continued to hold the four physicians in high esteem and lavished on them favors and gifts, in part, because they were terribly afraid of them. The Europeans were surprised by the exaggerations, lies, and fear that came with success in their labor among the sick. On the other hand, they decided to try to take advantage of it so they could keep moving. Cabeza de Vaca put it like this:

"[The runners and guides told those in the next villages that we were children of the Sun. They must not] hide anything ... because this would not be [done] without our knowing it and then we would cause all of them to die. ... The Sun [would] tell us. [As to some] so great were their fears aroused that during the first days that they were with us, they never stopped trembling and did not dare to talk [to each other] nor to raise their eyes to the sky . . . Through all that land ... [they] became so frightened of us that it seemed that [just] from the sight of us, they would die of fear. They begged us not to be angry, nor to will that more of them should die; and they believed that certainly we [could] kill them merely by wishing it."[411]

The same path through these lands, from Toyah Creek to the Rio Grande, taken by Cabeza de Vaca and his party in 1535 was followed in 1583 by the group of Antonio de Espejo with his assistant Diego Pérez de Luxán on their way back to New Spain.[412] From the village of Recepción close to the mouth of Toyah Creek, they walked about thirty-three miles, or eleven leagues, upstream to a gushing spring, undoubtedly one of those near the Texas town of Balmorhea. Then, they marched forty-eight miles, sixteen leagues, through a "sierra," the Davis Mountains, by means of two wooded "canyons" or "valleys" each with a stream, Madera Creek, running through it.[413]

The Davis Mountains do not fit Cabeza de Vaca's description of the arid, "rough mountains" with no game. Unique in the region, this scenic "sky island" receives more rain than the surrounding desert and has trees, creeks, and many pronghorn antelope, mule deer, and other animals. In 1535, Cabeza de Vaca and his party ascended upstream Madera Creek through the long, narrow Madera Canyon. Passing over the divide, probably north of Mount Livermore's summit, which rises to an elevation of over 8,000 feet, Cabeza de Vaca walked out to see the north-flowing Wild Horse Draw. Later, Espejo would ride a horse through the same area.[414]

They next hiked about twenty-four miles, or eight leagues, over a wide grassy area, the Marfa Plains, in which sit the Texas villages of Valentine and Marfa. Following Wild Horse Draw to the south and then up an arroyo that flows from Capote Peak, their guides could have taken rabbit or antelope to roast for the travelers. Although still in the desert, there is no mention of thirst because the trail always followed the running water of streams.

After crossing the Marfa Plains, Cabeza de Vaca walked past a site where there were some pools of fresh water. The explorers then trekked eighteen miles, or six leagues, over "bad trails through" a "very rough" sierra.[415] These were the Sierra Vieja, the dry mountains of affliction that rise to an elevation of 5,000 to 6,000 feet. Here the four physicians were stalled by hunger and illness.[416]

The trail followed the flow of two creeks pouring down from the slopes of Capote Peak that is a height of just over 6,200 feet. The group ascended beside the stream that flows north from the summit where there are occasional light showers. The trail

138

descended alongside the other, Capote Creek, that flows south before turning west. The point of arrival at the Rio Grande was near the mouth of Capote Creek about three miles north of the tiny Texas village of Candelaria.

Cabeza de Vaca and the other Spaniards were exhausted from the climb through the dry mountains, measured by Luxán to be eighteen miles from the entrance to the Sierra Vieja around to the mouth of Capote Creek. In the plains, it would have taken only one day of walking, but there in the arid sierra, the four had to stop to work with their many patients. Of hundreds in the caravan "there was hardly anyone who was not ill."[417] The four Spaniards, who saw this interruption as a "very great trouble," were kept busy. It appears they went up to three days without food.[418] With Cabeza de Vaca as their model, they saw it through.

Finally, after the sick got better, and after they trudged over the rugged grey and reddish-brown rocks and cliffs of the Sierra Vieja, the four *físicos* arrived at the waters of the great blue river that was handsomely dressed on both banks in a band of green trees and brush. The flood plain alongside the river supports a thick growth of reeds, mesquite, willows, and groves of cottonwood trees.[419]

They approached the river and looked over to the opposite bank but did not cross there, despite the inexact wording of Cabeza de Vaca who suggests that they did. Instead, they probably turned left because it is expressly stated that is what Espejo did in 1583. Both groups followed the established Native American trail that went downstream through the sites of the tiny Texas villages of Candelaria and Ruidosa.[420]

The span that Cabeza de Vaca and party trekked to the banks of the great river from the Toyah Creek mouth, on the shortest route that followed creeks, was about 123 miles.[421] They walked to the southeast through the narrow strand of green that gradually widened into a treeless, grassy area of "some plains at the end of the mountains." Here, the flood plain stretches out west of the Chinati Mountains so as to slope gently down toward the river.

Then it becomes almost flat on both sides, carpeted, after the late summer rains, with short, green prairie grasses.[422] Continuing some twenty-seven miles downstream from the Capote Creek mouth to the river bank opposite the isolated mountain, Cabeza de Vaca completed the 150 miles of the Candelaria Trail.[423] He and his group waded across at the established indigenous ford and entered the nearby village that the Spaniards named San Bernardino.[424]

On the far side of the river, they were welcomed by the local inhabitants and met others who had come from far and near. The four travelers treated the ill and, once again, were presented honorariums, food, and a small hut in which to spend the night.[425] At San Bernardino, as at Recepción, the bags of food, arrowheads, and such that formerly had been stolen, were presented directly to the four *físicos*.[426] The Spaniards immediately distributed them to their guides from the last village. Strangely, many of the gifts were abandoned on the ground and left to waste.[427]

From here, the four *curadores* did not go north along the Rio Grande, as frequently asserted. They had *arrived* from the north and crossed the Rio Grande at San Bernardino, about fifteen miles north of La Junta de Los Rios (at the Conchos mouth).[428] When he remembered this last crossing, Cabeza de Vaca described it as a *Rio Muy Grande,* a very big river, "that came up to the chest."[429] From Río Hermoso, Cabeza de Vaca and his companions had traveled "many days," up to thirty-five, following their native guides, some 610 miles on foot to the north and then south to the great river.[430] Aware they had survived the crisis of the dry mountains, they now began to look and listen for any sign of other Europeans.

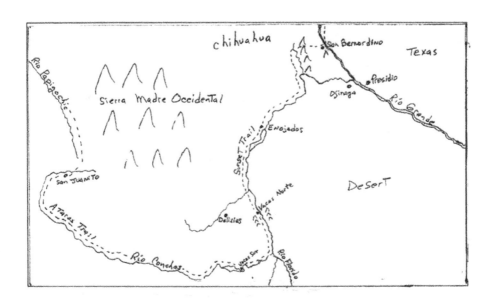

Map 18- ACROSS NORTHERN MEXICO. After they forded the great river for the third and final time at San Bernardino, they followed the Sunset Trail across the mountains then south and upstream the Conchos before they stopped at Enojados. Here they waited for the women to return from Vacas Norte, the Jumano village on a river between mountains.

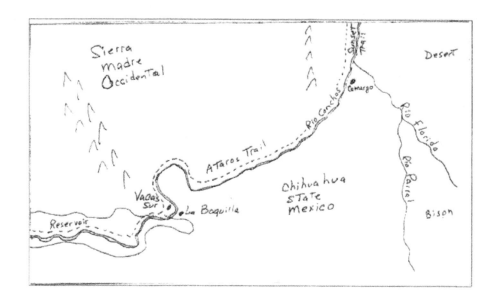

Map 19- THE WAY TO THE NORTH. At the village of Vacas
Sur, the Jumanos pointed downstream the Conchos, which was
from there "to the north" and to the bison in the region of the two
rivers, the Florido and the Parral. The Jumanos were not saying that
the bison were somewhere to the north but that the trail started out
in that direction.

Chapter 14
Upstream the Conchos

Neither Cabeza de Vaca nor the others knew where they were. They wanted to go west, but undoubtedly the native people kept telling them they could not go that way. The Europeans had no knowledge of the terrain, the distances, or of whether those in the next village would be hospitable. They may as well have been blindfolded. In every direction, there were either strange, unknown mountains or hundreds of miles of desert plains. In places, the land seemed to extend into the distance without end. Completely dependent on the local people, they had no more than the vaguest idea how to arrive at the Pacific coast.

Esteban, who was the first African slave to live in the United States, was appointed to communicate by signs with local residents when the four arrived at a new settlement.[431] Having become a true European, he was highly regarded and was given the important responsibility of a spokesman and mediator. Like the other Spaniards, he wanted to go "home" where he could get on with the rest of his life. At San Bernardino on the Rio Grande, he would have had one crucial question: Which trail should we take to arrive at the lands near the western ocean? He and the other European travelers desperately wanted to go to the Pacific coastal plain, in northwest Mexico, where they knew the Spanish conquerors had begun to build some small towns.[432]

Dorantes was especially anxious to find other Spaniards, and he was now getting tired of the daily grind of walking through one long trail segment after another. He could be impatient with the other Europeans and also with the indigenous people. Likely, the native guides had annoyed him with the stop in the dry mountains of affliction. Then, when they finally arrived at San Bernardino near the ford on the Rio Grande, he must have been agitated when there was confusion and conflict as to which trail to take.

While the natives of San Bernardino pointed at two roads to the coast, there was a big problem with each. On one long stretch of the way "to the north," the Casas Grandes Trail, there was no water, people, or food.[433] This road started upstream on the right bank and split away from the Rio Grande, possibly near Cajoncitos, about seventy-five miles southeast of El Paso. It then passed through the desert, probably, and went by the ruins of Casas Grandes, an abandoned city also called Paquimé, and upstream along the Río Casas Grandes to the region of Yepomera.[434]

Having followed their guides mostly northbound for several hundred miles from Platita, near Los Ramones, Nuevo Leon, to Recepción, near Pecos, Texas, Castillo, Esteban, Dorantes, and Cabeza de Vaca were finished with going "to the north." Having recently suffered through the dry mountains of affliction, the Sierra Vieja, they also were finished with arid, uninhabited regions with no food. As a result, they chose the Sunset Trail, the second option presented, which followed a small stream west from San Bernardino, then went up and over some mountains, the Sierra El Peguís. "Very far" down this trail, the next village, Vacas Norte, sat on the banks of a "river that runs between mountains," and the sierra slopes were close to the water's edge. Unfortunately, the village was a community of their ferocious enemies, the Jumanos.[435] Cabeza de Vaca called these natives the "people of the cows" because they hunted the bison.

While the Native Americans of San Bernardino feared the bellicose Jumanos and did not want to go to their village, Cabeza de

Vaca and his companions insisted on this path. They were thinking, mistakenly, that it would continue directly to the west and to the sea. The four Spaniards did not realize that on the other side of the mountains, the Sunset Trail meandered, not west but south, more than 150 miles along the Río Conchos before it turned back to the west at Camargo.[436]

Cabeza de Vaca gave an account of the exchange with the local people at San Bernardino on the Rio Grande:

"By signs, we told them we wanted to go toward the sunset… they answered that in that direction, the next village [Vacas Norte] is very far away. We asked them to send runners ahead to notify them that we were coming. Because those [Jumanos] were their enemies, they did not want us to go to them. But since they did not dare do otherwise, they sent two women, one of theirs and another whom they had captured. Women can barter even if there is war between communities."[437]

The Jumanos had a reputation as fighters who frightened other bands. It was not at all clear they would be friendly even if the four strangers were healers who promised to tend to their sick and injured. Cabeza de Vaca and the others already had lived with hostile communities in Arboleda on the lower Guadalupe River where they were compelled to labor as slaves. They had turned away from the path to Pánuco because they were warned of violent-prone people who lived down that way.

Since the local people did not wish to go to the enemy village, they sent the two women in place of the usual four male runners.[438] At a certain point on the way, the two women separated themselves from the main group and went ahead to see if the Jumanos would welcome the Spaniards. Meanwhile, the others of San Bernardino guided the four Spaniards over the mountains to Enojados, a site about a three-day walk of sixty-to-seventy miles from the village.

Records of two Franciscan missionary expeditions of the early 1580s reveal the path of the Sunset Trail that the four *curadores* took, in the opposite direction from the village, in the fall of 1535. The group with the Franciscan missionary Agustín Rodríguez (d. 1582) departed Santa Barbara near Hidalgo de Parral in June of 1581 and traveled north along the Río Parral, the Río Florido, and the Río Conchos. Antonio Espejo and his group came up on the same route the year following.[439] As they approached the region called La Junta de Los Rios, also known as the Ojinaga Valley, the area near the Conchos mouth, they veered away from the Río Conchos. They were blocked by the Cañon del Peguís and by the surrounding mountains.[440] After marching due north a few miles from the river, they turned to their right to climb over the heights of the Sierra El Peguís whose peaks are over 6,000 feet above sea level. On the far side, they trekked some ten miles east along a creek to its mouth on the Rio Grande where there was a native village they named San Bernardino. It sat at the base of an isolated mountain that rises to about 4,200 feet.[441] About fifteen miles north of the Conchos mouth the mountain is named El Ramireño and locally it is called El Cerrito.[442] From this village of San Bernardino on the Rio Grande, Cabeza de Vaca and his party took this same road in reverse.[443] They followed the mountain creek, El Arroyo Seco, and spiraled up into the Sierra El Peguís. On the far side, they turned left, southbound, to follow another creek that joined the Río Conchos.[444]

On multiple occasions on this epic journey, Cabeza de Vaca survived only with the assistance of indigenous women. When he was in the lands opposite Malhado-Galveston Island, the wife of Principal may have helped him recover from his sickness. Some Deaguanes women ferried him and Lope across Matagorda Bay and San Antonio Bay to the pecan groves on the lower Guadalupe River. Two women forded the great river and hiked north to Cincuenta Sur to beckon the famous *físicos* to their hometown of Calabaza near Ciudad Mier in Tamaulipas. Now, two women messengers from San Bernardino, one of whom was a prisoner of war, went before them down the Sunset Trail as intermediaries to attempt to make for a peaceful entrance into the Jumano village of Vacas Norte.

After an overnight stop at Enojados in the region of the reservoir Luis L. Leon, also called Lago El Granero, in eastern Chihuahua, the Spaniards wanted to keep going forward; but the guides would not take another step toward the Jumanos.[445] This refusal angered the frustrated Spaniards, especially Dorantes. Even Cabeza de Vaca was upset and bewildered. Making the situation even worse, the two women who had been sent ahead to the enemy village did not return as agreed. Had they been held against their will? Would the Jumanos be hostile toward the four *físicos?*

For a second time, a fear of this mysterious tribe of Jumanos formed a barrier to the four European men. If the Jumanos of Vacas Norte would not give them a friendly welcome, perhaps they should turn back to follow the path, the Casas Grandes Trail, that ran upstream the Rio Grande from San Bernardino. This would require them to retrace their steps for seventy-to-eighty miles and then go still farther "to the north" along the right bank of the great river. Their guides did not want to do this because somewhere out there on a long segment of that path there was no water, they repeated by signs, or people, or food.

With its giant loop north into Trans Pecos Texas, the route taken by the four may at first look strange on a map, but it makes sense. They were following established indigenous footpaths alongside freshwater streams from the east to the west side of the Chihuahuan Desert.[447] The four were not engaged in a leisurely search for the richer nation as some have said.[446]

When their guides from San Bernardino refused to advance beyond Enojados toward the Jumanos, angry Dorantes made some ill-natured threats, warning their native companions they should perish for their recalcitrance. He and the other Spaniards had seen enough of these vast Far Away Lands in Texas and northern Mexico. It was now early November of 1535 and they began to sense that, at last, they were getting close to the South Sea, the

Pacific Ocean, and, hopefully, to other Europeans. They wanted no more delays.

"We are very far away" from our homes, the native people responded. "The tunas have ended. We are very hungry."[448] We want "to stay" or "go somewhere else," they told the bearded ones. They wished to travel neither forward nor back to San Bernardino and then to the north to Casas Grandes. Filled with fear and dread, "more than three hundred" of their travel companions fell ill and "many died."[449]

We are not surprised that Dorantes lost his temper; but Álvar Cabeza de Vaca also became agitated. It was a rarity for him since he was always giving thanks. This is the one place in the narrative of the journey that reveals an ugly side of all four European travelers. Dorantes attempted to frighten their guides into doing something they did not want to do, and Cabeza de Vaca followed him in this. He refused to provide his healing services and went alone into the country to pray and think. No doubt he now felt the same desperation as when his expedition was stalled in Florida years before:

"[It seemed that we were in] a land so strange and so evil and so lacking in help for anything, either for remaining there, or for getting out of it. But … the surest help is God our Lord, and of him we never despaired … In order to leave [such a land] and to seek some way out, for [it appeared that] there was none, [while some fell ill and others…were dying]… and seeing these… difficulties, and having tried many remedies, we agreed on one… [to minister to the native people while we waited to see what may occur]."[450]

The Spaniards expected the two women messengers to arrive at the end of only one day after they stopped at Enojados.[451] When the expectation was not met, Dorantes got angry. On the third day, the women finally walked up with the "very bad news" that an appropriate celebration was not possible because most of the men of the village were off hunting bison. Also, there was not much

148

food due to a drought. Nonetheless, the four Spaniards were welcome to enter and to pass through Vacas Norte and their other Jumano villages farther down the trail. Disinterested in the festivities, the *físicos* wanted only to keep moving to the Pacific coast.[452] Still nervous about drawing near to the warlike Jumano people, Cabeza de Vaca hastily worked out a plan of approach. The sick would remain at Enojados and only "twenty or thirty of those who were well were to go with them" on to the village. Castillo and Esteban would go to the village with the two women and gather some of the Jumanos to come out to meet Cabeza de Vaca and Dorantes on the road.[453] After three more one-day trips, they dismissed the guides. The next day they walked about eighteen miles, entered the village, and the crisis finally came to an end.[454]

Cabeza de Vaca observed, as did Espejo and Luxán, that the Jumanos constituted a large tribe of handsome people in several "clusters of villages.[455] "This land is very populated," he recorded, and these people had "the best bodies that we saw."[456] Davenport and others have proposed that from the region of the Conchos mouth near Ojinaga and Presidio, the four traveled upstream along the Rio Grande to El Paso and across southern New Mexico. However, many years after the epic journey of 1535 these same Jumano people indicated that the Cabeza de Vaca group traveled south upstream along the Río Conchos, not north.

As they guided the Espejo party through their string of settlements, one after another, all the way up to San Bernardino, at each stop the Jumanos communicated fond memories of how, forty-seven years before, "three Christians and a Negro had passed through their land."[457] In 1581-82, several of the Jumano settlements sat at intervals along the northernmost length of the lower Río Conchos, roughly between Camargo and Ojinaga. When Espejo recorded that the Jumanos accompanied the Spaniards along "the banks of the river for a distance of twelve days' travel," he was referring to the Río Conchos, *not* the Rio Grande as commonly thought. If the four physicians were traveling along the

Rio Conchos between the Florido mouth and the Conchos mouth, they were going broadly south upstream, not north downstream. They would not have crossed the desert from the Sierra de la Gloria to arrive at the area of the Rio Florido mouth.

Over four decades later, the Jumanos were still talking favorably about the brief, but cherished, visit of Cabeza de Vaca and the other three. By sharing this information, the Jumanos inadvertently revealed that, from San Bernardino on the Rio Grande, the Cabeza de Vaca party headed west to cross the Sierra El Peguís, then south along the Río Conchos to the Río Florido mouth at Camargo and beyond.[458] The Jumanos, who were called "naked" by the Spaniards because they wore only a few pieces of bison leather, were a large tribe with several clusters of settlements on the banks of the Río Conchos.[459] They built permanent houses, grew corn, squash, and beans, and hunted the bison in Mexico.

Cabeza de Vaca in 1535, and Espejo in 1582, although arriving from opposite directions, first met the Jumanos at the same place - the village of Vacas Norte on "a river that runs between mountains." Cabeza de Vaca and his party came down from the north, while Espejo rode in from the south. In a mistake repeated many times, Davenport placed this Jumano village near the Río Conchos mouth on the Rio Grande where both rivers flow through a desert floodplain and not between mountains. The village of Vacas Norte sat, in fact, where the Mexicans later built a reservoir, the Presa Rosetilla, in Chihuahua, a few miles east of the town of Delicias.

In 1535, the territory of the Jumano people "of the cows" ran along the Río Conchos south and southwest from this village of Vacas Norte at the Presa Rosetilla, where the river really does run between mountains. Rising to about 4,500 feet above sea level, with some peaks off the left bank to the west and others off the right bank to the east, the rugged heights of a range of mountains enclose the river. This is a narrow valley in which the slopes rise steeply from both banks.[460] In 1582 when Espejo went through, the

Jumanos had migrated to the north to establish several villages at intervals in the riparian lands that later ran between Camargo and Ojinaga.[461]

Cabeza de Vaca began to have some level of excitement and hope when he noticed the Jumanos seemed to be more advanced, with, for instance, real, "permanent houses." These were flat-roof dwellings, in distinction from the portable, tent-like huts of various types in which other indigenous groups spent the night. The Jumanos were traders who knew well the roads that led to distant sites. When they communicated to the four traveling Spaniards how they grew corn when there was rain, and that on the far side of the mountains, there was a coastal plain in which the people grew lots of it, the four Europeans' hearts must have jumped.[462] At last they appeared to be drawing near to their interim destination on the west coast. Now they began to watch for any sign that they were getting close to the towns of New Spain.

Cabeza de Vaca relates that indigenous groups "who were at war with others would … become friends" as result of the visit from the four *físicos* who then "left the whole land at peace."[463] Between 1535 and 1581, it appears that the Jumanos, after making peace with other indigenous groups who lived on the Rio Grande near Presidio and Ojinaga, introduced them to permanent houses and taught them to raise corn and vegetables. Meanwhile, the Jumanos acquired the clay pot, which it appears they did not have in 1535.[464]

When the four healers met them in 1535, many of the Jumanos of Vacas Norte had "gone to the cows," or to hunt bison, at a site about ninety miles away. In addition to the tasty meat, they also used bison body parts to make bowstrings, tools, and blankets. Based in part on an unfounded presumption that in Mexico there were no bison, Davenport, like others, placed the Jumano village of Vacas Norte on the Rio Grande at La Junta de Los Rios. He assumed that the bison hunting grounds were also in Texas.

At Vacas Norte, the Jumanos told Esteban and the other Spaniards that, both "near" there and at other places "upstream that river," the Conchos, and up to 150 miles, or fifty leagues distant, their men went to hunt the bison. Only ten-to-twenty miles to the west at Delicias there was a wide expanse of grassy fields adjacent to the Río San Pedro - a place for the bison that was "near." The herds also could have grazed in the plains seventy to ninety miles away at Búfalo on the Río Parral and in the region of Jiménez on the Río Florido. About 150 miles "up" the Río Conchos, the Río Florido, and tributaries, there were areas near Villa López and Escalón in Chihuahua and Ceballos in northeastern Durango with seasonal grasses.[465]

Reports of large bison herds located to the south and west of the Rio Grande in the 1530s and the 1580s have been corroborated by studies of the historical and the archaeological record. Ancient specimens such as bison bones have been found. Such authentic records tell us that the "historic range of the bison included northern Mexico."[466]

Cabeza de Vaca was the first outsider to write an eyewitness description of the bison, and he tells us he saw the herds three times, possibly including in northern Mexico. In that the indigenous people who lived near the Sierra de La Gloria gave the four physicians bison blankets, they must have hunted them in the nearby lands of eastern Coahuila and northern Nuevo Leon.[467] In October 1866, Lew Wallace, author of the novel *Ben-Hur,* went hunting among hundreds of bison between some hills north of Parras in southern Coahuila.[468]

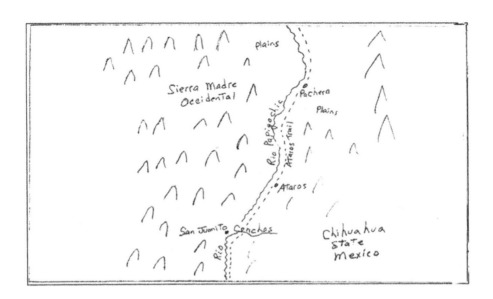

Map 20- THE PASS OVER THE CONTINENTAL DIVIDE.
From Vacas Sur, the Ataros Trail continued to the west and then
turned north to San Juanito where, to go over the continental
divide, they "had" to cross the Rio Conchos and follow tributaries
of the Rio Papigochic into the "plains between some very big
mountains."

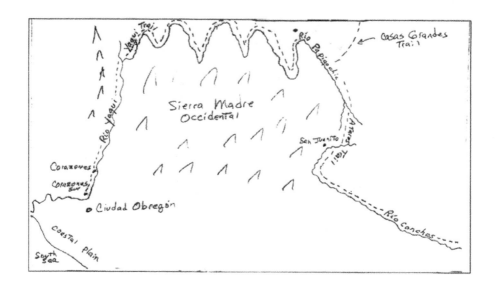

Map 21- THE YAQUI TRAIL. They continued north into the Papigochic Valley to the area of Yepomera where they turned west then south now to follow downstream the tributaries of the Rio Yaqui to the coastal region. The two villages of Corazones and Corazones Sur were just north of the site of the city of Obregón.

Chapter 15
Downstream the Papigochic and the Yaqui

In the fall of 1535 Álvar Cabeza de Vaca and his three companions hiked through the precipitous river valleys of the Sierra Madre Occidental until they entered Corazones, *hearts*. After a few days, they walked down to Corazones Sur. To the point of arrival at these two villages on the Pacific coastal plain, it appeared the native people knew nothing about other bearded Europeans and the triumph of Hernán Cortés over the Aztecs in 1521. If the flooded Río Yaqui had not forced the four to stay two weeks at Corazones Sur, they may not have seen the man there who had a Spanish belt buckle and a Spanish horseshoe nail hanging around his neck.

These two little pieces of metal, worn as a distinct necklace, were the first indications that the four were indeed drawing near to New Spain. Wanting to know where and under what circumstances these objects were obtained, Cabeza de Vaca and his companions, while being careful to avoid revealing their identity, coaxed out of the local people bits and pieces of an account. Certain bearded men had appeared, perhaps months earlier, coming up from the nearby sea in the west alongside the river. The strangers, who had swords and lances, seized as many natives as they could, probably killing some in the process. Those whom they took away in their big ship were never seen again.

Some thirty-five days before their arrival at Corazones, the four travelers were at Vacas Norte, the Jumano village a few miles east of the town of Delicias on a "river," the Conchos, "that runs between mountains." They were searching for the best path to the far side of the rugged sierras to the west.[469] Perhaps to make up for the earlier delays in the Sierra Vieja, the dry mountains of affliction, and at Enojados, the place of anger, the Spaniards resumed a rapid pace through a string of four large Jumano villages. These "clusters of towns" sat at intervals along the trail that followed the Río Conchos upstream.[470] Passing through the verdant riparian strip near Ciudad Camargo, the four would eventually walk into the Papigochic Basin at its southern terminus to follow downstream the Río Papigochic.

One of the Jumano clusters, Vacas Sur, must have been located in the area of the Chihuahuan town of Boquilla de Las Babisas on the banks of the Conchos near where later arose the dam of the large reservoir the Presa La Boquilla.[471] To walk from this village back to the mouth of the Río Florido and beyond, a traveler had to go almost due *north* a few miles with the flow of the river and then, after a dog-leg, to the northeast several more miles. From here, to indicate the path to the bison herds, the Jumanos pointed north parallel to the downstream path of the river. Hence, the record says the bison were located "to the north;" although, in fact, they were likely at a site to the southeast, on the Río Florido and Río Parral, in the region of Ciudad Jiménez and Colonia Búfalo.[472]

The four stayed a second night at Vacas Sur, probably in mid-November of 1535. They needed more time to make a choice about the route through the mountains to the land of much *maíz*, corn, near the seashore. Unknown to Cabeza de Vaca, between here and there, these steep mountains of the Sierra Madre Occidental were an enormous barrier to travelers. There were no east-west passes. Other than to walk a long distance to the north or south to go around the mountains, the only way through was the crooked path alongside the tributaries of the Río Yaqui.

Meanwhile, the Jumanos, who had no horses, gave the Spaniards a little lesson about the Spanish word *maíz* that may have had a structure something like the following:

"For two years we have not grown it here because of a severe drought. Please ask your God to make the clouds pour out rain. The maíz we offered you came from the far side of the mountains toward the sea at a place that is to the west and yet also to the north. On the plains up and down the coast, the people grow lots of it. We went there to trade our excellent bison hides and returned with bundles of corn on our shoulders."[473]

The Jumanos assumed the four were looking for villages, which, like theirs, had plenty of food and more sick patients to touch and bless. They warned there would be few people and a dearth of food if they continued upstream alongside the nearby Conchos river and downstream the other rivers, tributaries of the Yaqui. For the Spaniards to meet many more friendly people with plenty to eat, the Jumanos recommended the "way to the cows" that started "to the north" from this village.[474] By lifting hand and arm toward the north, the Jumanos were suggesting a route that turned back along the Conchos from where the four had just come.

The road "to the north" from there led both "to the cows," which was not so far, and eventually to the Pacific coastal region of much corn that was "very, very far," the Jumanos confessed. The shorter route to the western sea was upstream "that river," the Río Conchos, on the path they were already treading. The Jumanos were recommending the road that took them back north by northeast to the mouth of the Río Florido at Ciudad Camargo. The Spaniards had marched past this trail that, from there, meandered broadly to the south through high passes and valleys to Mexico City. By another fork, it reached one of the rivers that fed into the Pacific Ocean, perhaps the Río Santiago. [475]

Not interested in following any more roads "to the north," the Spaniards instead chose what appeared to be the shortest route to the sea, which from there was again "toward the sunset."[476] On the left bank of the Río Conchos, this trail took them through the valley of Zaragoza, where probably sat the last in the string of Jumano villages. From there, they continued until, about twenty miles southeast of Bocoyna, the path turned more to the north for almost 100 miles before twisting west again. This is the reason the Jumano people told them it was a trail both "to the north" and "to the west."[477]

Álvar Cabeza de Vaca and the others hiked up into the mountains alongside the Conchos, whose upstream path turns back to the east to its head or source. The Continental Divide, over which the four Spaniards must pass, lay a few miles to the north from where they "had to cross" near the little town of San Juanito.[478] They now entered lands where the rainwater flows no longer into the Río Conchos or the Rio Grande and on to the Gulf of Mexico but into tributaries of the Río Papigochic, the Río Yaqui, and on to the Gulf of California.

Both narratives refer to a unique landmark through which they soon passed—some plains "between very big mountains."[479] About a one-day journey north of the spot where they forded the Conchos, they entered an expanse of open country with green hills and gently sloping pastures. These plains, which are called the *Llanos de la Reforma*, are a stretch of grassy fields about sixty miles long and, in places, up to ten miles wide. These open meadows are indeed between great, high sierras with peaks over 8,500 feet both to the east and to the west. Through this region the party trekked north until, near the village of Yepomera, the Río Papigochic and the trail alongside it turns west into the sierras.[480]

While they made several changes in direction as they followed downstream the tributaries of the Río Yaqui, they were still traveling broadly to the west.[481] More than likely, Cabeza de Vaca, with his garbled reference to two travel segments of seventeen days each, intended to express something like the following:

"At the end of about seventeen days of walking [from Vacas Norte], we crossed the river [the Conchos]. Then we continued for

158

another seventeen days in part through an area of grassy plains between some large mountains. Although the trail led us north and then south, we worked our way broadly toward the setting sun until we arrived on the other side of the sierras at Corazones where there was a lot of corn."[482]

The reality on the ground tells us that the two travel segments of seventeen days each started at Vacas Norte just east of Delicias, from where they walked four-to-six days, to Vacas Sur near Boquilla de Las Babisas.[483] After two more days, they came to the final Jumano cluster of towns, likely in the fertile Valle de Zaragoza. The two references (to a travel segment of nine-to-ten days just before they crossed the Río Conchos) refer to the span from the Valle de Zaragoza to the Conchos ford. As we will see further on, this may have been the home of the Jumanos, named by the Spanish the Querechos, who, in 1565, rushed over to see Francisco de Ibarra and his party near Yepomera at the northern end of the Papigochic Basin.[484]

They passed through narrow, forested valleys where, as they had been warned, there was only a little to eat, consisting of "powdery straw," some "hares," and "deer fat."[485] In the hope of soon arriving at the place of an abundance of *maíz*, Cabeza de Vaca and his party pressed ahead on a zigzag route in cool regions along the Río Sirupa and the Río Aros to the mouth of the Río Bavispe. They then traveled south down into hot country where the Mexicans later built two large reservoirs on this same Río Yaqui.[486]

Because it was the first major village they encountered after coming out of the mountains onto the coastal plains where the local people cultivated *maíz*, Cabeza de Vaca described it as "the gateway," *la entrada*, to that part of the country.[487] He also called it Corazones, or hearts, because here, after the prayers and ministrations for the sick, the local people gratefully presented Dorantes a large quantity of dried deer hearts, which were considered a delicacy. Well into the twenty-first century sportsmen came from far and near to go hunting the many deer in this region bounded roughly by the Río Concepción, the Río Yaqui, and the coast. [488]

Still on the right bank of the Yaqui, for three days at Corazones, the *físicos* rested and offered their services before going south to Corazones Sur. At the latter village, the river "grew" so much from recent rains that for fifteen days, they were not able to cross. The village of Corazones Sur sat thirty-five to forty miles from the coast, where, just north of Ciudad Obregón, the southbound Río Yaqui turns more to the west. If the village of Corazones was "a day's journey," or twelve-to-twenty miles to the north, then it likely was located on ground later covered by the waters of the lake, the Presa Alvaro Obregón.[489] Oviedo recorded that the two villages were thirty-six to forty-five miles, or twelve to fifteen leagues, from the sea. This evidence renders the conventional site for Corazones, at Ures on the Río Sonora, another error, for Ures is more than ninety miles from the shore.

Some thirty years after the epic journey of Cabeza de Vaca, Governor Francisco de Ibarra (1539?–1575) with his assistant Baltasar de Obregón (1540?-1590?), launched an exploratory journey along these same rivers. Ibarra wanted to find what Coronado did not, the large, rich city or nation of Cabeza de Vaca that Ibarra believed sat in the "northern boundary" of his province of Nueva Viscaya.[490] The *Chronicles* of this expedition in 1565-66 provide corroborating evidence that the four *físicos* indeed took this route through the high plains along the Río Papigochic and from there down the valleys of the Río Yaqui river system to the village of Corazones. If the four traveled north through the Papigochic Basin, they also followed, from Trans Pecos Texas, trails that ran upstream the Río Conchos to the region not far from its head, as set forth here. Because of intervening mountains, there is no other practical way to enter the southern end of the Papigochic Basin on foot.

After departing Culiacán, Ibarra and his group languished for weeks in the hot climate near the Río Yaqui delta unable to cross

160

the mountains. Upon finding two local guides, they worked their way to the lush high plains at the northern end of the Papigochic Basin. In his *Chronicles* of the expedition Obregón described their route, which was the same, although the reverse of that of Cabeza de Vaca in 1535. On a path of less difficult passage because it followed the river valleys between the "slopes," they worked their way to some notable "plains" in a "cold" climate. After resting for several weeks, they found a path from there north to the ruins of Casas Grandes.[491] These features can refer only to the high plains of the Papigochic Basin where, at an elevation of about 6,000 feet, it is cold at night but warm most afternoons year round.

After Ibarra and Obregón made a right turn out of the last of the rugged, steep mountain valleys, they rode their horses up into the heights to look across a verdant, open grassy region. Ibarra and his companions were struck by the grandeur of "the rolling hill country carpeted in grass and fringed by mountains" with "arroyos, streams, and smaller rivers" that fed into the Papigochic before it makes its "sharp turn into the sierra."[492] Here in the Papigochic Valley were the plains between large mountains recorded in both narratives of the journey.

The account of some days on the trip in this area near Yepomera to Casas Grandes, Paquimé, is an unequivocal identification of both sites, the plains along the Río Papigochic and the site of the abandoned city near the modern town of Nuevo Casas Grandes. Ibarra followed the Río Casas Grandes downstream where he and his party were the first non-natives to see the ruins of the civilization that thrived roughly AD 1200 to AD 1450.

While Ibarra, Obregón, and company were taking several weeks of rest in the region at the northwest terminus of the Papigochic Valley or Basin, they encountered two separate indigenous groups who gave voluntary attestations of having met, in these very lands, Cabeza de Vaca in 1535. Those of a nearby band "assured" Ibarra that there were many cures when the four men passed through, probably at this same site. "On account of" their fond memory of the "deeds and happenings" associated with Cabeza de Vaca, they treated Ibarra and his companions well.[493]

Then some of Ibarra's soldiers captured a young man from a distant native community. After he calmed down, Ibarra gave him a shirt and pants and sent him away. Later, by perhaps three or four weeks, the young man returned with some 300 men, women, and children from his home village. Obregón recorded that these bison-hunting Querechos, who came singing and dancing, did not live there in the high plains. Rather, they had come from afar, probably from the Valle de Zaragosa, while the Spaniards were recuperating.

The Ibarra Querechos described "others" who, in "appearance," were like Ibarra and Obregón, that is, not brown but white or black and bearded. Having "passed through their lands years before," they "had caused their enemy to return captives whom they had taken, … had ordered the clouds to rain on their lands, had healed the sick, and resurrected the dead."[494] There was no doubt to Ibarra and Obregón that they were talking about Cabeza de Vaca, Esteban, Dorantes, and Castillo.

This report of the Ibarra Querechos, who met the explorers during their expedition of 1565-66, corresponds to the 1535 visit of the four *físicos* among the Jumano people along the Río Conchos. Like the Querechos, the Jumanos hunted the bison; one of the Jumano women who had been a prisoner of war was sent back to her home; they implored Cabeza de Vaca and his companions to ask their God to send rain after a two-year drought; and the four Spaniards had undoubtedly tended to their sick.[495]

As Cabeza de Vaca and his companions traveled through the Papigochic Basin, then over to the two villages on the lower Río Yaqui, the adulation that started at Cincuenta had preceded them. Here in these regions, the local people also offered them generous tokens of appreciation for the healing services that Cabeza de Vaca had first learned on the Isla de Malhado. The grateful inhabitants of Corazones presented the Spaniards the dried deer hearts, beads, and coral from the nearby Sea of Cortéz.

To Cabeza de Vaca they also gave five green arrowheads which he thought were made of emeralds. However, emeralds were rare in Mexico; moreover, they are brittle and not usually cut up or molded into various forms. The gemstone from which the arrowheads were formed was probably the widely available jade or jadeite, many of which were luminous green (like emeralds) and more malleable for shaping.

Impressed with the craftsmanship and the beauty of the stones, Cabeza de Vaca inquired into their origin. They had been obtained, so they were told by signs, in trade for certain "feather bundles" and "parrot plumes" at a large, wealthy city. At the site of this mysterious, rich city, high in some mountains, there were busy markets and more "towns" of "many people" with "very large houses."[496]

In *Historia General* Oviedo added some lines that described this same rich nation. It was a site "of many people and much food, …cotton and … houses [that were] large." Also "they had many turquoises," meaning such items as the green arrowheads, that were available "by trade."[497] The four Spaniards realized this was the same rich nation or city with very tall houses described to them earlier at Cascabel. From here, the rich city was said to be "toward the north" on a sea with many permanent houses and artisans who worked with molten metal to make ornaments including copper rattles.[498]

Along with the others, Cabeza de Vaca caused a stir in Mexico City when he arrived in 1536 and innocently passed on what he understood about the rich city in the distance. First, Marcos de Niza with Esteban, in 1539, and then Coronado, in 1540, proceeded north to Arizona and New Mexico in an extensive search for this big metropolis. However, among the Pueblo people they met in New Mexico, there were only small towns with no large markets and no artisans who worked with molten metals. Despite a long side trip into Texas, Oklahoma, and Kansas, Coronado failed to find the large, rich nation; he then returned to Mexico City which was precisely where it had been all along!

In Cascabel and Río Hermoso in northeastern Mexico, and later at Corazones Sur in northwestern Mexico, the local people had told the truth about the rich nation. The Native American people of these villages did not yet know in late 1535 that the wealthy Aztec city had been destroyed in 1521. They knew nothing about how, during a great siege with many fierce battles, the Spaniards had conquered the rich city and then had built *Ciudad de Mexico*, Mexico City, on its ruins. Before they were destroyed in battle, large edifices, including several high pyramid temples, rose from the impressive city of Tenochtitlán. The big Aztec city was situated at an elevation of over 7,000 feet in the basin of Mexico, on some islands in a "sea" or a set of connected lakes.

At Tlatelollco in the northern part of the city, there was a large market where merchants offered cotton blankets, tools, decorative objects, and other products. The Aztecs were fond of colorful feathers such as those that had been traded for the five green arrowheads. Artisans worked with molten metals to make artistic items such as engraved copper rattles like the one given them at Cascabel. While they had turquoise and other gemstones, green jade was the "single most valuable material to the Aztecs," and from it they made ear plugs, bracelets, and other objects, such as the five decorative arrowheads.[499]

The road to the wealthy nation of the Aztecs ran first north from Corazones Sur along the Yaqui Trail recently traversed by the four physicians; later, it turned south and upstream at the mouth of the Río Florido near Ciudad Camargo. From there, it meandered south to Tenochtitlán, possibly following, in part, predecessor trails of the *Camino Real de la Tierra Adentro*. The same as at Cascabel in northeast Mexico, here at this village on the Río Yaqui in northwest Mexico, when the local people were asked about the site of the wealthy nation with large cities, they pointed "toward the north."

The preferred trail to Tenochtitlán in the Valley of Mexico started out that way, as it happened, from both places.

From the day they escaped the violent slaveholders of the region near San Antonio, the four travelers had assiduously kept away from any contact with other such cruel people. They had decided to turn inland from the region of Cerralvo to avoid the hostile people who lived toward Pánuco. Yet after crossing the Río Yaqui and going parallel to the Pacific coast toward Culiacán, they again encountered a tribe of avaricious slave hunters who were committing acts of violence and creating chaos. Ironically, these cruel slavers were men of their own Spanish tribe! The first European *conquistadores* that Cabeza de Vaca met were heartless men who made money by enslaving hundreds of the native people. They sold these human beings to those who would compel them to work and suffer in the silver mines or on Caribbean plantations.

From the beginning, Cabeza de Vaca had "many and very great quarrels" with the slave hunters. He tried to defend the 600 indigenous people who, still filled with adulation and admiration for the four, were traveling with him. He would not permit them to be arrested. He may have fought this battle alone, for there is nothing in the record to suggest that Dorantes and Castillo felt as strongly against slavery and mistreatment of the indigenous people. The royal treasurer knew that, under Spanish law, it was illegal to arrest them without an opportunity to cooperate, convert, and to work peaceably with the Europeans.

Some years later, the conflict over treatment of the indigenous people followed Cabeza de Vaca to a province in South America - Paraguay. As governor there in the 1550s, he tried to implement humane and Christian policies by which the native people were to be treated with respect as human beings. However, the Spanish settlers, wanting nothing to do with such policies, trumped up various false charges and had him arrested and sent back to Spain in chains. Although he lost at trial, he prevailed on appeal and spent the last years of his life in Spain, as far as we know, in relative prosperity and peace.[500]

The *físicos* survived the long trek across the continent to Corazones and beyond. Among other reasons for this success is the fact that, on the shores of Malhado, after his sobs and prayers, Cabeza de Vaca made friends with the Native Americans. They trained him to be a physician and a merchant and thereby prepared him for the long journey. During the first years in the lands of *los montes* along the Colorado and Brazos rivers of Texas, he was given a warm welcome in each successive village. For almost two years in Arboleda and Aransas, the lands near San Antonio Bay, and in Nopales, the place of prickly pears near San Antonio, he was a mistreated slave; however, he continued his healing services. After their last miserable winter in the United States, with the Avavares in the lands of Los Rios on the Nueces River, the Europeans made their way to the far south Texas village of Cincuenta. Here, his work in the healing arts lifted Cabeza de Vaca and the other three into a lofty social status. His cures and reputation safely propelled him and the others across the continent until, in the Pacific coastal plain of northwest Mexico, he met other Spaniards.

Despite the dismal conflict with the slave hunters who came at the end, Cabeza de Vaca, along with Dorantes, Castillo, and Esteban, arrived at last in New Spain. After living about a half year in Florida and almost seven years in Texas, they had successfully concluded an epic, overland journey of survival, overcoming many obstacles. The *físicos* made the long trek across the continent from Malhado to Corazones and beyond, and they did it with compassion. Under their able leader, the men found a way to serve the native people. Up to forty-five years later, the indigenous people were still talking about the four travelers' brief visit in their lands and the healing power of their touch.

The four Europeans entered the region northwest of the city of Culiacán in Sinaloa, and after the dispute with the slavers, they eventually departed and were escorted to Mexico City where they were received as heroes. Viceroy Antonio de Mendoza soon sent Esteban to his death in 1539 on the expedition of Marcos de Niza. Both Dorantes and Castillo married wealthy widows and stayed in New Spain. Cabeza de Vaca returned to his wife in Spain where he wrote and published his book *Los Naufragios*.

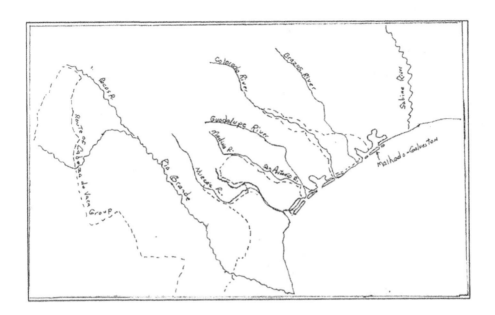

Map 22- THE ROUTE THROUGH TEXAS. The broken line
indicates the approximate route taken by Cabeza de Vaca who
began the epic journey by walking west by northwest from
Malhado-Galveston Island.

About the Author

Dr. Lawrence D. Sharp is an independent researcher who has spent many years studying the journey of Cabeza de Vaca across North America. He is a lawyer in private practice in Dallas, who has been a speaker in churches and at gatherings of lawyers. Holding both a Doctor of Ministry in church history from Vanderbilt and a Juris Doctor from Tulane, he brings a unique perspective to this captivating story. He contends that the other books are wrong at key points and has compiled a positive narrative that reveals how Cabeza de Vaca survived (with three others) and where he really was in the long overland voyage from the island of Malhado on the coast of Texas to the village of Corazones in northwest Mexico.

Notes

Chapter 1

1. Álvar Núñez Cabeza de Vaca, *Los Naufragios*, in Krieger, Alex, <u>We Came Naked and Barefoot</u> (Austin: Univ. of Texas Press, 1999), p. 179; Rolena Adorno and Patrick C. Pautz, <u>Alvar Núñez Cabeza de Vaca</u>, Vol.1, (Lincoln: University of Nebraska Press, 1999) pp. 94-97; several words are used interchangeably for Native Americans including the indigenous, the Amerindians, the local people, etc.

2. *"Nuestro miedo los hazía parescer gigantes."* Rolena Adorno and Patrick C. Pautz, <u>Álvar Núñez Cabeza de Vaca</u>, Vol.1, (Lincoln: University of Nebraska Press, 1999) p. 94; also in Alex D. Krieger, <u>We Came Naked and Barefoot</u> (Austin: University of Texas Press, 2002), p. 179.

3. Davenport, Harbert, and James B. Wells. 1918 and 1919. "The First Europeans in Texas, 1528-1536," <u>Southwestern Historical Quarterly</u> 22(2): 111-142 and 22(3): 205-259, [accessed online 1/28/2009 at] http://www.tshaonline.org/shqonline/apager.php?vol.022&page 121.

4. In <u>We Came Naked and Barefoot</u> Alex Krieger provides a translation of the 1555 edition of the *Los Naufragios* or <u>The Shipwrecks,</u> and also of *Historia General* or the <u>General History</u> (the shortened titles used here). I have also used the translation of the 1542 edition of <u>The Shipwrecks</u> of Adorno and Pautz, as well as their transcription of the Spanish text. Cabeza de Vaca did not make any substantive changes when he published the later 1555 Valladolid edition *La Relación y Comentarios del gobernador* Álvar Núñez *Cabeza de Vaca*, of which Maur says it is *"básicamente igual a la edición príncipe (*Zamora, 1542*)."* Juan Francisco Maur, ed., <u>Naufragios of Álvar Núñez Cabeza de Vaca</u>, (Madrid: Catedra Letras Hispanicas, 2010), p. 63.

5. Oviedo's narrative is based on the *Joint Report* or sworn statement attended and attested by three of the survivors (all except Esteban); it appears that the official in charge let Dorantes do most of the talking.; Adorno and Pautz acknowledge that Oviedo committed errors of omission and "confusion" in his desire to eliminate material he considered to be repetitious and superfluous. Adorno & Pautz, pp. 20-27.

6. By means of a mountain pass that he had marked with a cow's skull, a *cabeza de vaca*, Martin Alhaja, a maternal ancestor of Cabeza de Vaca, is said to have led a Christian army through a mountain pass to a place where they won a victory over the Moors; his paternal grandfather, Pedro de Vera, conquered the Canary Islands for Spain. Keith Brandt, *Cabeza de Vaca: New World Explorer* (Troll Associates, 1993).

7. Adorno and Pautz, Vol. I, pp.17-19.

8. This part of the voyage is well described by Andrés Reséndez in <u>A Land So Strange</u>, (New York: Basic Books, 2007), pp. 62-90.

9. Krieger, p. 180-186.

10. In the fall 1539, those of the Soto expedition found near the shore of Apalachee Bay, possibly upstream from the Ochlockonee mouth, "the remains of" the camp where Narváez had built his log boats "for the desperate trip along the Gulf coast." Cf. Paul E. Hoffman, <u>A New Andalucia and a Way to the Orient</u> (Baton Rouge: Louisiana State University Press, 1990), pp. 91-92.

11. Krieger, pp. 179-181.

12. Davenport; it is clear that it was Davenport, not Wells, who was primarily responsible for the research and drafting of these articles.

13. Diego Perez de Luxán, in his account of the Espejo expedition of 1582-83, gives the travel spans of each day along the Conchos from the Florido mouth to the Rio San Pedro; in 6 days they made 60 miles (a total of 20 leagues or 3.0 miles per); with a 2.6 mile league the distance would come to 52.0 miles (8.0 short); Diego Perez de Luxán, "The Account" (of the Espejo expedition 1582-83), edited by G. Hammond and A. Rey, <u>Rediscovery of New Mexico 1580-1594</u> (Alberqueque: Univ.of New Mexico Press, 1966), pp. 155-156; Krieger, p. 43-44.

14. Juan Bautiste Chapa used a 3.0-mile league when he states the distance from the old city center of Saltillo to that of Monterrey was 18 leagues, a span

of about 54 miles that, by the early 2000s, had not changed since the late 1500s. Juan Bautista Chapa, "Historia del Nuevo Reno de Leon," translated by Ned F. Brierly and edited by William C. Foster, <u>Texas & Northeastern Mexico: 1630-1690</u> (Austin: University of Texas Press, 1997), p. 53.

15. Krieger, pp. 180-186, 255-263; Marie Beth Jones, "San Luis, Texas," in <u>The Handbook of Texas Online</u>, at <u>http://www.tshaonline.org/handbook/online/articles/SS/hvsem.html</u>.

16. About 1785, Spanish explorer José de Evia is said to have named it after Bernardo de Gálvez. Cf. <u>www.citytowninfo.com</u>; An artificial channel has been dug for the ICW canal which separates Folletts from the mainland; a few have held, mistakenly, that Malhado was Marsh Island in Louisiana, or perhaps San Jose Island farther down the Texas coast. Cf. Donald E. Chipman, "Malhado Island," <u>The Handbook of Texas Online</u>, at <u>http://www.tshaonline.org/handbook/ online/articles/MM/rrm1.html</u>.

17. Krieger, pp. 180-186.

18. Krieger, p. 180. If there were swells large enough to break the log raft in two, it would not have been an easy swim to shore.

19. "We were begging our Lord" (*estuvimos pidiendo a nuestro* se*ñor),* Adorno & Pautz, Vol. I, p. 98.

20. Krieger, pp. 180-181.

Chapter 2

21. Krieger, p.182.

22. Krieger, p.170.

23. In both original narratives,*atrás,* or "back," refers to the east or northeast toward the Florida peninsula from where they had come, whereas *adelante,* meaning "ahead" or "forward," refers, (as does "toward Pánuco" and "inland"), to the direction that was generally to the west. *Ibid*, pp. 186, 210.

24. To match accompanying maps, I have given names to the various regions, important villages, and trails described in the two narratives.

25. Krieger, p. 191-193.

172

26. Krieger, p. 191-193.

27. After a third barge wrecked near the mouth of Caney Creek, the governor had to ferry the men down to (probably) San Jose Island where their journey came to its tragic end. Krieger, p. 191-193.

28. Krieger, p. 186.

29. *Handbook of Texas Online,* Priscilla Myers Benham, Texas City, TX, www.tshaonline.org/handbook/online/articles/hdt03; also *Wikipedia, Texas City, Texas,* Wikipedia.org/wiki/Texas_City,_Texas.

30. Dos leguas por lo mas ancho del aqua, Adorno & Pautz, p.116.

31. References from the Spanish edition of *Historia General* by Oviedo y Valdez are in The Journey of the Vaca Party, transcribed and translated by Basil C. Hedrick and Carroll L. Riley (Carbondale, Illinois: Southern Illinois University, 1974), p. 112 & p. 259.

32. The journey of the Dorantes Group down the Four Rivers Trail to Arboleda was of only a few days duration (in early April 1529), although the narrative here stalls to give some details; in the early 2000s at low tide, Drum Bay was only 1-2 feet deep, Bastrop Bay 2-3 feet, and Christmas Bay was (in most places) 2-4 feet deep; these depths were taken from the Galveston Island Nautical Chart (publisher unknown) that was on display August 17, 2010, at Galveston State Park office.

33. Krieger, p. 187.

34. Krieger, p. 259.

35. Krieger, p.258-259; Hedrick & Riley, p. 112.

36. Krieger, p. 191, and p. 259.

37. Clearly, it was not Cabeza de Vaca who gave this testimony, for in his own account, he shows no interest in these distances; since these were approximations of the kind that sometimes err on the low end, the span from the River One mouth to that of River Four will likely be from 40 to 50 miles. Krieger, pp. 259-261.

38. Krieger, p. 259, and p.191. In the 1800s and earlier, Oyster Creek flowed all the way to the ocean before it was re-routed to flow into the Intracoastal Waterway canal.

39. Following Davenport, Alex Krieger mistakenly asserts that at the time of Cabeza de Vaca, Oyster Creek was "about nine miles from the Brazos" mouth and that the latter was the second river not the first. Neither was aware that, as part of a port development plan 1926-29, the Brazos mouth was artificially moved to free the former mouth as a seaport facility (part of the Freeport Harbor Channel); starting at the Gulf end in 1926, the new channel was excavated and constructed so as to put the river mouth nine miles to the southwest; this meant that the old channel could serve without interruption as a deep water port, free of accumulating dirt or silt which rendered it too shallow for large seagoing merchant ships and tankers. Based on information personally provided by my friend Glen Heath of Freeport, Texas. Krieger, p. 37.

40. Krieger, p. 112.

41. Krieger, p. 191 and p. 259.

42. Nor did they return to Malhado from the mainland opposite, for this would have required that they cross a third bay or ocean channel from Malhado to Folletts and from a theoretical southwest tip of Folletts prior to the six-mile walk to River One, a scenario not indicated in the narratives.

43. In times of drought, the San Bernard does not quite reach the sea. Cf. Walden, Janice Van Dyke, "The San Bernard River Once Again Flows to the Sea," Texas Highways, March, 2010, (Austin: Texas Dept Transportation), p.34; clearly these distances are estimates; we are looking for comparisons, not specific accuracy; the witness, probably Dorantes, is saying that if Distance Two was about ten miles, then Distance Three was longer by perhaps a half to a full league, or 1.5 to 3.0 miles.

44. Krieger, pp. 260-261; the third river could not have been Cedar Lake Creek because the distance to it from the San Bernard would have been only about five miles, instead of the nine to twelve of the record, and the fourth distance would be a little too far.

45. Clay, Comer, and Diana J. Kleiner, "Colorado River," in The Handbook of Texas Onlinehttp://www.tshaonline.org/handbook/online/articles/CC/rnc10.html

46. Krieger, pp. 260. The narrative mentions that it was on the fourth day of the trek down the beach that the Dorantes group arrived at the large bay, i.e. Matagorda Bay.

47. There is nothing in the two narratives to suggest that the survivors

started their journey on Bolivar Peninsula or somewhere east of Galveston Bay.

48.Krieger, p. 191. Cabeza de Vaca says that Dorantes traveled 15 leagues, or 45 miles, "further on" where they "found another bay"; and *Historia General* in Krieger, pp. 260-261 records they went twelve leagues, or thirty-six miles, and then saw a second bay. Near Port O'Connor, a fresh-water creek flowed east into the bay; it would have been the logical site for an overnight stop at about the halfway mark of the canoe trip from the east end of Matagorda Bay to the mouth of the Guadalupe River.

49. Krieger, p. 181. These proposed sites are consistent with the narrative which states that, from the barge of Cabeza de Vaca, the men were taken a "far" distance (of about three miles?) that first night in the cold to the Capoque village. A site that was four or five miles northeast of there in Han territory would have been located somewhere near the end of 53rd Street in the city of Galveston.

Chapter 3

50. Krieger, p.188.

51. In a quote from the *Joint Report*, he is referred to as "one of their leaders" or, in archaic Spanish, *"un principal dellos."* In later usage, "principal" is mainly an adjective, not a noun. Hedrick and Riley, p. 109.

52. Krieger, pp. 185-186.

53. Cabeza de Vaca did not become a "shaman" or "witch doctor" since he neither adopted any primitive religious beliefs, nor did he attempt to placate powerful spirits; he merely adopted Amerindian rites, practices, and remedies and coupled them with European Christian prayers.

54. Based on the testimony of Pierre and Jean-Baptiste Talon in "Voyage to the Mississippi," translated. by Linda Bell and annotated by Robert S. Webber, in La Salle, the Mississippi, and the Gulf, (College Station: Texas A&M University Press, 1987), p. 238.

55. Throughout this work, I have expanded minimally, and paraphrased freely, so to clarify what I believe he truly intended to say. Krieger, p.184.

56. According to an exhibit on display at the Jamaica Beach City Hall on August 10, 2016, the Jamaica Beach archaeological site was accidentally discovered in November 1962. T. E. Pulley and Charles Butler directed the dig

in which some nineteen skeletons were found as well as a flint knife, pottery, arrowheads, and other artifacts. A carbon-14 test indicated that some of the remains dated to the early 1500s.

57. "Mitchell Ridge," at the Texas Beyond History website, http://www.texasbeyondhistory.net/mitchell/investigations.html .

58. Krieger, pp.182-186.

59. Un indio que a mí me tenía. Adorno & Pautz, p.106.

60. *Una enfermedad de esto mago.* Adorno & Pautz, p.106.

61. Gary Cartwright, <u>Galveston, A History</u> (Fort Worth: TCU Press 1991), p. 17.
62. Lyle Saxon, <u>Lafitte the Pirate</u>, (Gretna: Pelican Publishing Company, 1999), pp. 220-221.

63. Alice W. Oliver, "Notes on the Carancahua Indians," edited by Albert S. Gatschet, <u>The Karankawa Indians, the Coast People of Texas,</u> (Cambridge, Mass.: Peabody Museum, 1891), pp. 16-20.

64. The prehistoric burial site was discovered in 1962 at Jamaica Beach only two miles west of the site at Mitchell Ridge. Cf. www.Texasbeyondhistory.net /mitchell/investigations.html.

65. Robert A. Ricklis, "Cabeza de Vaca's Observations …" at the website of the Center for the Study of the Southwest, http://swrhc.txstate.edu/cssw/resources/cdvwindows/ricklis.php; Cf. also "Mitchell Ridge," at the Texas Beyond History website, http://www.texasbeyondhistory.net/mitchell/investigations.

66. Davenport and Wells, p. 121. The island is neither thirty-nine miles in length using the faulty gauge of 2.60 miles for each of the five leagues (X3) nor forty-five miles using the correct three mile measurement.

67. "it is in the nature of sand bar – barrier islands to be continually shifting shape, size, and position over the centuries and millennia, so it is possible (but not necessarily guaranteed) that the west portion of the island could have been separate at one time, before recorded history; it is also possible that no one may know whether this was actually so …",private email from Peter J. Modreski of the U. S. Geological Survey, Denver, Colorado, August 13, 2007. pmodreski@usgs.gov.

68. Robert A. Morton, "Historical Changes in the ... Barrier Islands," <u>Open File Report 2007-116 U. S. Geological Survey</u>, (St. Petersburg, Florida: U. S. Dept. of the Interior, 2007); www.pubs.usgs.gov./of/2007. The print of its widest fifteen-mile segment appears to have remained substantially the same despite several artificial alterations. After the hurricane of 1900, they pumped tons of silt to build a rampart in the form of a seventeen-foot seawall that sloped from the top to the bay shore. While Galveston Island was growing at its other end, the "island behind" the record that later became the site of East Beach, also grew at its southwest tip to add some 3.5 miles.

69. S. C. Griffin, <u>History of Galveston, Texas</u>, (Galveston: A. H. Cawston, 1931), p. 19. Francis C. Sheridan recorded in 1840 that Galveston ranged "from one to two" miles in breadth. Francis C. Sheridan, edited by Willis W. Pratt, <u>Galveston Island, Or, A Few Months off the Coast of Texas 1839-40, The Journal of Francis C. Sheridan</u>, (Austin, University of Texas Press, 1954).

70. Davenport and Wells, p. 121. At three representative points spread out down the island length, at Rosenberg Street, Pabst Road, and Jamaica Beach, it is indeed very close to 1.50 miles wide.

71. It is doubtful that Lope, from an eye-level of eighteen to twenty feet up a typical island tree, could have seen both ends; but he could see the bay behind and that it appeared not to be connected to the mainland in either direction; hence, he quickly announced that it was an island. Most of the wild trees that grew on the seashore side of the island (before Hurricane Ike in 2008) would not have been tall enough to climb any higher.

72. William C. Davis, <u>The Pirate Lafitte</u>, (New York: Harcourt Inc. 2005), p. 353-354.

73. Francis C. Sheridan, "Galveston Island, Or, A Few Months off the Coast of Texas, 1839-40" in <u>The Journal of Francis C. Sheridan</u>, edited by Willis W. Pratt, (Austin: University of Texas Press, 1954), p. 32.

74. Sheridan, pp. 120-121.

75. Krieger, p. 187 & pp. 257-258. I consulted briefly with Sonia Kania, professor of Spanish at the University of Texas at Arlington.

76. Davenport and Wells misunderstood the references to "the woods." When Cabeza de Vaca states he departed for the region of the woods, or "*los montes,*" he was referring to the forested areas along the Brazos, the San Bernard, and the Colorado rivers farther to the northwest, not to the area along the shore of West Bay; even farther up Halls Creek still in the early 2000s, there

were thick stands of large trees. Cabeza de Vaca had to carry loads of firewood either in these "woods" or on Malhado itself. Cf. Davenport and Wells, *Ibid.*

77. *Una islaatrás,*Hedrick and Riley, pp. 112, 259. Kriegeer, pp. 257-258.

78. Cf. a good map of Galveston Island is <u>Galveston/La Marque/Texas City: A Five Star Map,</u> (Carbon, Texas: Five Star Maps, Inc., 2006).

79. The Island Behind was not likely either Pelican Island (in the wrong place) or "Little Campechy" (probably a sand bar that washed away). Davis, pp. 397-398.

80. At low tide, the local adult men, in an emergency, could possibly swim or wade across, but with children they needed canoes; the Spaniards did not want to attempt to go three miles with their bags and swords in water up to five to six feet deep. Francis Sheridan observed in 1840 that north of the city, Galveston Bay was twelve to fifteen feet deep (i.e., at places to the north and northeast of downtown at the time) which may be contrasted to Drum Bay, Christmas Bay, and Bastrop Bay, the lagoons adjacent to Folletts Peninsula which, for the most part, range from one to four feet in depth at low tide. Sheridian, pp. 32, 44.

81. The Amerindians did not live there in large numbers in the summer; even so, the summer heat is tempered by the sea breeze and frequent rain showers.

82. Cf. William C. Davis, <u>The Pirates Lafitte: The Treacherous World of the Corsairs of the Gulf,</u> (New York: Harcourt Inc. 2005), p. 308. In sandy areas near the beach such wells may yield brackish water, but in the areas of dense growth of canes, especially toward the bay side, fresh drinking water was available in this way; Terry G. Jordan, et al, <u>Texas: A Geography,</u> (Boulder, Colorado: Westview Press, 1984), pp. 18-19.

83. Sheridan, p. 121.

Chapter 4

84. Krieger, p. 187.

85. Krieger, p. 186.

86. Krieger, p. 199.

87. Krieger, p. 185.

88. Krieger, p. 185-186.Cabeza de Vaca circulated for three years in the coastal plains of Texas roughly enclosed by a line from Galveston to Houston to Austin to Matagorda and back to Galveston.

89. Krieger, p. 187.

90. Krieger, p. 188. Cabeza de Vaca called the whole of the lands of the forested rivers "Los Montes," while the segment along the Brazos was called "Charucco."

91. Krieger, p.188.

92. Krieger, p. 188.

93. Some think that in the period of 1630-1650, the Amerindians of the southern Plains began to acquire Spanish horses. Wallace, Ernest, & Hoebel, E. Adamson, The Comanches: Lords of the South Plains, (Norman: University of Oklahoma Press, 1952), pp. 33-39.

94. Talon, Pierre and Jean-Baptiste, "Voyage to the Mississippi," in LaSalle, the Mississippi, and the Gulf, edited by Robert S. Weddle, translated by Ann Linda Bell, (College Station: Texas A&M University Press, 1987), p. 230.
95. Krieger, p.187.

96. For example, the "nuts," or pecans, were said to be "on the edge of that river." Krieger, p. 189.

97. Krieger, p.196. Another reason to reject Folletts-San Luis Peninsula is it shows no signs that it has ever had many trees; it is a mostly treeless landmass.

98.Krieger, pp. 184, 187.

99. Krieger, p. 188.

100. Adorno &Pauck, p. 120.

101. Cf. The Roads of Texas, (Addison, TX: Mapsco Inc., 2008).

102. Cantrell, Gregg, Stephen F. Austin: Empresario of Texas, (New Haven: Yale University Press, 1999), p.202.

103. Or twenty-three to twenty-four leagues. Krieger, pp. 258 and 187. Since Cabeza de Vaca would not have said that he went "sometimes inland," this part

of the testimony must be from the mouth of Dorantes.

104. Dalton Garrett, Daphne, "Fayette County," The Handbook of Texas Online, s.v.http://www.tshaonline.org/handbook/online/articles/FF/hcf3.html,.

105. Krieger, p. 198.

106. Krieger, p. 189.

107. Krieger, p. 188.

108. Weddle, Robert S., San Juan Bautista Gateway to Spanish Texas, (Austin: Univ. of Texas Press, 1968), p. 125 ff.

109. The French explorer Jacques Cartier (1491-1557) was in Canada in 1534, while Cabeza de Vaca was still living in the United States.

110. Krieger, pp. 208-210, 220.

111. Cabeza de Vaca mentions most of these animals in connection with the passage through the Florida peninsula; Krieger, pp.166, 188.

112. *Tierra tan despoblada*, Krieger, p. 152; Adorno and Pautz, Vol. I, p. 100.

113. Krieger, p.. 188.

114. Oliver, Alice, in Gatschet, Albert S., The Karankawa Indians: The Coast People of Texas, (Cambridge, Mass.: Peabody Museum, 1891), pp. 17, 60; Diego Perez de Luxán is another example of a Spanish explorer of that age who considered a person "naked" or even "completely naked" if they wore only a little clothing that minimally covered the genitals for, writing of the expedition of Antonio de Espejo in 1582-83, he described a band of natives whom they met as "naked people," yet in the same sentence he indicated that what he meant is that they are people "who cover themselves with skins of rabbit and deer" and that the women cover themselves likewise "but not their breasts." Of the Jumanos along the Conchos, Luxán wrote that they "go practically naked," but he quickly added that what he means is that "they cover themselves with well-tanned skins of the Cibola" or bison. Diego Perez de Luxán, "Account," in Rediscovery of New Mexico Vol. III, translated and edited by George P. Hamond and Agapito Rey, (Albuquerque: University of New Mexico Press, 1966), pp. 155-156; 160-165.

115. Adorno and Pautz, Vol. I, pp.18-20.

116. Adorno and Pautz, Vol. I, p. 22; cf. p. 207 of Robert S. Weddle, Spanish Sea, (College Station: Texas A&M University Press, 1985).

117. "*Sin razon y tan crudos a manera de brutos,*" Adorno & Pautz, Vol. I, pp. 100-101.

118. Krieger, pp. 182-183. From his record of this incident, it is apparent that Cabeza de Vaca did not know about it until they had already died, and hence, the five would not have been from the group on his barge.

119. Krieger, pp. 228, 234.

120. Krieger, p. 228.

121. Krieger, p. 228.

122. Krieger, p. 234.

123. From about October 1532 through all of 1533 and another nine months of 1534.

124. Krieger, p. 188.

125. Krieger, p. 201.

Chapter 5

126. Krieger, p. 189.

127. Krieger, p. 188.

128. Krieger, p. 210. Cabeza de Vaca writes from the perspective of the lower Guadalupe River, which puts the two large bays "behind" them; he uses different spellings for Deaguanes because he was trying to put a native word into Spanish letters; hence, we have the "Deaguanes," the "Doquenes," the "Aguenes," etc. He does the same with his references to the Capoques.

129. Krieger, p. 189. The mound on which sits Port O'Connor was at about the midway point and, with a creek nearby and some trees, would have been a perfect place to put up a camp for the night.

130. Krieger, p. 189.

131. Krieger, p. 189.

132. Krieger, p. 189.

133. On the right bank, not far from the coast, there was some higher ground still in the early 2000s with trees; in the salt-water bays, the native people could fish and gather oysters; a short distance to the north, they could hunt deer, and there was fresh drinking water in the Colorado River.

134. Krieger, p. 189.

135. Krieger, pp. 188-190.

136. These descriptive factors are not consistent with placing Arboleda at Cedar Bayou, the strait that separates San Jose Island from Matagorda Island where there are no pecan trees and no rivers.

137. Personal letter from L. J. Grauke to the author by e-mail dated June 7, 2008. Dr. Grauke is an adjunctprofessor of Horticultural Science at Texas A&M University. Cf. the website at http://aggie-horticulture.tamu.edu/carya/people/lj04.htm. On a short walk along the right bank of the Guadalupe River north of the small town of Tivoli in May2008 and a drive down the road toward the mouth of the river, my son Brenan and I saw the levee and found that many of the pecan trees had been removed years before.

138. Krieger, p.189.

139. Krieger, p. 190.

140. Krieger, pp. 189-190.

141.Krieger, p. 190.

142. Krieger, p. 190.

143. Over 150 years afterward, some French survivors of the La Salle expedition of the 1680s testified exactly the same as Cabeza de Vaca that those who "inhabit the seashore," referring to Amerindians of this same region, were "a people much crueler and more barbaric" than "any of the other" groups of the interior, or farther to the north or west. Talon, Pierre and Jean-Baptiste, "Voyage to the Mississippi," translated by Linda Bell and annotated by Robert S. Weddle, in La Salle, the Mississippi, and the Gulf, (College Station:Texas

A&M University Press, 1987), p. 229.

144. Krieger, pp. 190-194.

145. Krieger, p. 193.

146. Krieger, pp. 190-194.

147. Krieger, p. 269.

148. Krieger, p.269.

149. Krieger, p. 261. After a few days, they no longer had the canoe because the man or woman who paddled them over hastened back home.

150. During their years in this region, the Spaniards would have walked with their native hosts through or near the sites of the Texas towns of Tivoli, Victoria, Cuero, Goliad, Falls City, Gonzalez, and Halletsville.

151. If the distance from the mainland opposite the northeast end of Malhado-Galveston Island is measured so as to include the canoe ride back to Malhado (about five to six miles), the walk down the island (ten to twelve miles), the trip across Bay One (three to four miles), walking over part of the mainland in the search for Cabeza de Vaca (seven to fifteen miles), then southwest across Chocolate Bay (eighteen to twenty miles), down the beach and across the four rivers (fifty to fifty-two miles), some walking in the search for a canoe (fifteen to twenty miles), the ride over the two bays (forty-five to fifty miles), some miles up the Guadalupe River (perhaps ten to fifteen miles), the total distance that the four had traveled on the ground and over bays and rivers to arrive at Arboleda could have been 162 to 194 miles and thus consistent with the estimate of 180 miles (or sixty leagues). Krieger, pp. 268-270.

152. Krieger, p. 270.

153. Krieger, p. 268. The reference to a span of sixty miles suggests that the northeast extremity of the migratory region must have been upstream the Lavaca River.

154. Krieger, p. 196.

155. Krieger, pp. 195-196; cf. Robert A. Ricklis, The Karankawa Indians of Texas: An Ecological Study of Cultural Tradition (2010: University of Texas Press, p. 97). Bison bones were found at the Melon Site near Copano Creek in Refugio County.

156. In the plain of Refugio, to the south and west of Austwell, cotton and other row crops were later planted and stretched as far as the eye could see.

157. Krieger, p. 190.

158. Krieger, p. 270.

159. Krieger, p. 272.

160. Krieger, pp.190, 199.

161. Krieger, pp. 190, 199.

162.Krieger, p.197.

163. Krieger, pp. 272-273. Six months prior to the departure for Nopales would mean late November for a late May departure to mid-December for a mid-June departure.

164. Krieger, p. 274.

165. Krieger, p.199.

Chapter 6

166. Krieger, p.197. The woman may have been a prospective wife.

167. Krieger, p.197.

168.Krieger, p. 273. "They could not communicate among themselves" during those months.

169. Krieger, p.197.

170. Krieger, p.197.

171.Krieger, pp. 190-191.

172. Krieger, p. 272 and p. 202.

173. Krieger refers to Nopales as "the tuna ground." Krieger, p. 41.

174. Davenport and Wells, 22(2): 111-142 and 22(3):205-259.

175. Krieger, pp. 197-199.

176. Krieger, pp. 272-273.Kingsville is only about six miles from a salt-water bay.

177. Krieger, p. 199. This will be explained in a later chapter.

178. Krieger, p. 198. There were actually many rocks beneath the surface under his feet.

179. Krieger, p. 271.

180. Krieger, p. 197.

181. Krieger, p.272.

182. Cf. Google Earth and the Texas Tech Digital Maps of Texas Counties.

183. Some of the local people who live in the hills along Highway 16, southeast of Somerset, told me they have their "own" prickly pear growing in their yards and, therefore, donot have to purchase them in markets. For many Mexicans and Texans, both the tuna and the thick green pads are a common food.

184. Cf. the Bexar and Wilson county maps in <u>Texas Almanac 2006-2007</u>, edited by Elizabeth Cruce Alvarez (Dallas: Dallas Morning News, 2006), pp. 167 ff.

185. Cf. the Texas Tech University Center for Geospatial Technology website at <u>http://www.gis.ttu.edu/center/</u> .

186. Krieger, pp.196, 198.

187. "Aunque hay rios, como nunca están de assiento, nunca tienen aqua conoscida ni señalada."Adorno and Pautz, pp. 150.

188. Krieger, p. 195.

189. Krieger, p. 202.

190. *Falta de otras vasijas.* Krieger, p. 150.

191. Krieger, p.150.

192. The Balcones Escarpment is a long geological fault that runs from the Rio Grande to the Red River; at San Antonio, it rises to about 300 feet and marks off roughly the northwestern third of Bexar County.

193. Krieger, p. 272. Oviedo recorded that they also "kill some deer sometimes," as at Aransas where they sometimes drove deer into San Antonio Bay.

194. Krieger, p. 196.

195. Quoted by Del Weniger in "Wilderness Farm and Ranch," in San Antonio in the Eighteenth Century, edited by Frances Hendricks, et al, (San Antonio: Bicentennial Heritage Committee, 1976), p. 100-102.

196. As quoted by Jesús F. De La Teja in San Antonio de Bexar, (Albuquerque: University of New Mexico Press, 1995), p. 112.

197. He wrote that it was a "*tierra muy frutífera.*"Adorno and Pautz, Vol. I, pp. 150-151; cf. Krieger, p 198.

198. "*Muy buenos pastos para ganados.*" Adorno and Pautz, p. 150.

199. Genetic analysis has shown that the Longhorns, brought to Texas by Franciscan missionaries in the 1600s, were direct descendants of some cattle brought over to the New World by Christopher Columbus in 1493. Dave Doolittle, "Longhorns' Texas Roots Run Deep," Dallas Morning News, (Friday, March 29, 2013), p. 3A.

200. Adorno &Pautz. p. 150.

201. Huddleston, Scott, "Historic Items Found near San Antonio River," Dallas Morning News, Sunday, Nov. 7, 2010 (originally published in the San Antonio Express-News), p. 5A.

202. "San Antonio de Valero Mission," in Handbook of Texas Online, s.v. http://www.tshaonline.org/ handbook/online/articles/SS/uqs8.html.

203. Chipman, Donald E., Spanish Texas: 1519-1821, (Austin: University of Texas Press, 1992), pp. 94-96.

204. Weniger, Del, "Wilderness Farm and Ranch," in San Antonio in the Eighteenth Century, edited by Esther MacMillan, (San Antonio: Clarke Printing

Company, 1976), p. 102.

205. Weniger, p. 102.

206. Theywere: Father Antonio de San Buenaventura y Olivares (circa 1650-1720) and Father Antonio Margil de Jesús (1657-1726). Donald E. Chipman, "Olivares, Antonio de San Buenaventura" (16?-17?), The Handbook of Texas Online, www.tshaonline.org/handbook/online/articles/00/fol4.html.[After over 180 years, the visit of the Royal Treasurer and his companions had faded from memory; moreover, they did not hold the Europeans in such high esteem as did other groups of Amerindians].

207.De Leon, Alonso, "Historia de Nuevo Leon," published and edited by Genearo Garcia in Documentos Ineditos o Muy Raros Para La Historia de Mexico, (Mexico: Editorial Porrua, S. A., 1975-reprint of the 1909 edition), p. 18.

208. Map of South Texas, (Corpus Christi: Texmaps.com, 2007).

209 Krieger, p. 213.

210. Krieger, p. 273.

211. Krieger, p. 197.

212. Krieger, p. 197.

213. Krieger, p. 197.

214. Krieger, p. 274.

215.Krieger, p. 274.

216. Krieger, p. 274.

217. Krieger, p. 274.

218.Krieger, pp. 197-198 and pp. 273-275.

219. Moonpage.com was accessed on September 21, 2016.

Chapter 7

220. Krieger, p. 274. They likely arrived at about 9:00 AM, CST, US.

221. Krieger, p. 274.

222. Krieger, pp. 197-198, and273-274.

223. Krieger, p. 274.

224. Krieger, p. 274.

225. Krieger, pp. 197-198, pp. 273-274. This will be explained in a later chapter.

226. Krieger, pp.273-274.

227. Krieger, p. 200. Robert Goodwin pays deserved tribute to Esteban in his essay. Robert Goodwin, Crossing the Continent 1527-1540, (London: Harper, 2008).

228. Krieger, p. 200.

229. Krieger p. 276.

230. Grant D. Hall, Steven Black, et el., "Archeological Investigations at Choke Canyon Reservoir…" and "Hunter-Gatherer Life along the Frio River in the South Texas Brush Country,"at the Texas Beyond History website, www.texasbeyondhistory.net/choke.

231. Krieger, p. 200.

232.Krieger, p. 202.

233.We assume that Castillo, like Cabeza de Vaca, at appropriate times, practiced, in addition to the prayers, cauterization, surgery, and herbal remedies. Krieger, p. 202.

234.Krieger, p. 199.

235. William C. Foster, Texas and Northeastern Mexico, 1630-1690, (Austin: Univ.Texas Press, 1997), p. 7. European settlers in Cerralvo, Monterrey, and

Monclova during the 1500s and 1600s reported that snow and ice were on the ground up to two months each winter.

236. During the "Little Ice Age" in the northern hemisphere, (which ran from about A.D. 1250 to A.D. 1850), the average daily tempature was some three to four degrees Farenheitcolder than, for example, in the late 1900s. Cf. "The Little Ice Age," at the website of the National Earth Science Teachers Association, http://www.windows2universe.org/earth/climate/little_ice_age.html .

237.Krieger, p. 199.

238. Krieger, p. 205.

239. Adorno &Pautz, Vol. I, p.156. Davenport does not address the issue of the five one-day journeys to the lands of Los Rios.

240.Krieger, pp. 200-201; Google Earth and the Texas Tech digital maps were helpful in finding this site. The Nueces is a sufficiently large waterway to have provided a home for several tribal bands, who, like the Avavares, migrated upstream and down. The Frio River, which does not have sections of multiple channels like the Nueces, must be ruled out (as the river of Los Rios) because it would have made no sense at all to travel downstream this river for several days, then to turn and retrace their steps to arrive at Los Ríos Dos and the second tuna ground.They did not travel downstream the Atascosa River to its mouth and then upstream the Nueces River (past the place of mesquite beans) to arrive at the region near the Highway 16 bridge because such a route would conflict with the series of events when Cabeza de Vaca got lost.

241. Krieger, p. 200-201.

242. Krieger, p. 201.

243. Charles Peguy, A Staircase for Silence as quoted by Walker at http://Solitary-Walker.blogspot.com /2011/01/walking-as-meditation-3.html (accessed on Feb. 26, 2011).
244. Krieger, pp. 200-201.

245. This site coincides with the five one-day trips to Cincuenta, the village of fifty huts, and the two thereafter to Cincuenta Sur and Calabaza, the village of the gourds (all to be explained below). Davenport does not deal with the five one-day trips from the Atascosa Campsite to Los Rio Uno, or the five journeys from Los Rios Tres to Cincuenta, the village of fifty houses.

246.Krieger, pp.203-204. Like his contemporary Michelangelo Buonarroti (1475-1564), Cabeza de Vaca was a devout, renaissance-era Christian who, although he produced nothing comparable to the art on the ceiling of the Sistine Chapel, wrote *Los Naufragios* as a colorful and lyrical account of how God led him through this odyssey of survival and adventure in the New World. He put more stress on that which was basic and ancient and less on the more complicated institutional dogmas and practices. His personal beliefs were in harmony with the call of Desiderios Erasmus (1466-1536) and others of the age for a return to the original simplicity of the creed, of prayer, of God the creator and redeemer, and of the basic moral commandments.

Chapter 8

247. Cabeza de Vaca in Krieger, p. 194.

248.Krieger,p. 194.

249. There is not a word in either narrative that suggests the Europeans hunted wild game on their own.

250. I used the maps and images provided by Texas Tech digital maps and Google Earth. The terrain in the hills of the Reynosa Plateau, between Freer and Guerra, would have been without trails and without water.

251. Krieger, p. 206.

252. Krieger, p. 206.They covered something like nineteen to twenty-two miles on the first travel-day (to the village of Maliacones), fifteen to seventeen on the second (to the village of Arbadaos), five to six on the third (to Arbadaos Dos), thirty to thirty-two on the fourth (to a camp on the trail), thirty to thirty-four on the fifth (to Cincuenta, the village of fifty houses now in Starr County), and six to seven on the sixth (to Cincuenta Sur). They slept on the path on the fourth night of travel for they found no villages in this segment of the Ygnacio Trail before they arrived at Cincuenta. The sixth jaunt to Cincuenta Sur was short and non-consequential, but the seventh will be described in more detail because it reveals where they discovered and forded what Cabeza de Vaca called a "great river" and, now on the Mexican side, entered Calabaza, the village of gourds.

253. The Reynosa Plateau is a line of hills, some over 800 feet, running north to south, mostly in the western part of Duval County, Texas. The first three travel days south from the Nueces River were done in about eight hours per day, with local guides at their side on the second and third days. On the fourth

and fifth they traveled more than the standard twenty or so miles; they had no Amerindians with them, and they kept going until dusk.

254. Krieger, p. 204. If Los Ríos Tres, the Avavares winter-spring campsite from which the four departed on the great overland journey, had been located substantially farther to the northwest or northeast from the mouth of Ygnacio Creek, more one-day trips would have been required than are given or implied in the narratives. In 1976-79. a young man and his new wife, who traveled by foot from New Orleans to the Pacific coast of Oregon, reported that in the hot sun of west Texas and while wearing out many pairs of shoes, they made about fifteen miles per day. Peter and Barbara Jenkins, *A Walk Across America*, <u>National Geographic Magazine</u>, August 79, Vol. 156, #2, pp. 194-229.

255. Krieger, p. 205.

256. Krieger, pp. 205-206.

257. Krieger, p. 205-206. Also, they may have been put on notice that: 1-the little creeks to the south may be dry, and 2- there were no villages within a one-day walk to the south.

258. Krieger, p. 205.

259. Krieger, p. 206.

260.La tierra es tan áspera y tan cerrada;Adorno & Pautz, pp.170.

261. Adorno and Pautz, pp. 171-173.

262. Krieger, p. 276.

263. Krieger, p. 206.

264. Krieger, p. 277. They may have walked 2.75 miles per hour. In June in South Texas if they left a half hour after sunrise, having eaten the cactus pads, they could have walked in daylight for twelve to thirteen hours.

265. Krieger, p. 277.

266. Krieger, pp. 276-277.

267. Krieger, p. 206.

268. <u>https://en.wikipedia.org/wiki/Coahuiltecan</u>, p. 5. Accessed Aug. 21,

2019.

269. Krieger, p. 277.

270. The five segments of this stream have been given as many names from north to south: Remadura de Charco Largo, Las Escobas, El Sauz, Las Blancas and Los Olmos Creek. The Roads of Texas, (Addison, Texas: Mapsco Inc., 2008), p. 158.

271. Krieger, p. 206.

272. Davenport, Harbert, and James B. Wells. 1918-1919. "The First Europeans in Texas, 1528-1536," Southwestern Historical Quarterly 22(2): 111-142; 22(3): 205-259; ,http://www.tshaonline.org/shqonline/apager.php? Vol. 022& page 228.

273. Krieger, p. 206.

274. The two original narratives use interchangably the Spanish terms *físico* (physician) and *curador* (healer).

275. Krieger, p. 232.

276. Krieger, pp. 205-206.

277. Adorno &Pautz, Vol. I, p. 165.

278. Cf. Robert Goodwin, Crossing the Continent 1527-1540, (London: Harper, 2008), pp. 150-151.

279. We will see this, for example, in the report of De León about the visit near Cerralvo in northeast Mexico, and also in the record of the Ibarra expedition in northwest Mexico.

280. Krieger, p. 212.

281. De León, Alonso, "Historia de Nuevo Leon," published and edited by Genearo Garcia in Documentos Ineditoso Muy Raros Para La Historia de Mexico, (Mexico: Editorial Porrua, S. A., 1975-reprint of the 1909 edition), p. 18. In the next chapter, the significance of the pass near the site of Cerralvo will be explained.

282. Cf. The Roads of Texas, (Addison, Texas: Mapsco Inc., 2008 www.mapsco.com), p. 158.

283. If the four passed southbound near Cerralvo subsequent to going through Calabaza, then the road they took must have run from the latter village to a point a few miles northeast of Cerralvo on tributaries of the Río El Alamo from the area near its mouth. Adorno and Pautz mistakenly say that the crossing was downstream from the Río San Juan mouth or below Rio Grande City. Adorno and Pautz, Vol. 1, footnote #1, p. 193.

284.Krieger, p. 278 and p. 213. The women caught up with the four about twelve miles from Cincuenta Sur, according to *Los Naufragios* or nine miles, according to *Historia General.*

285. This phenomena by which some Amerindian trails followed one creek upstream to near its head or source or beginning point, then, after passing over the divide, joined another so as to follow from its head downstream, will be discerned in the future route on at least four additional occasions.

286. They crossed the river *quando ya vino la tarde* and later entered the village *a puesta del sol.* Krieger, p. 278, p. 213; Adorno & Pautz, Vol. I, pp.193-194.

287. Krieger, p. 278. If in July in south Texas a person departs shortly after dawn (about 6:00 AM CST) and walks the full thirteen hours of available daylight, one could cover about thirty-five miles.

288. Based on a road trip through the region with my son Brenan Sharp in May 2008, in its natural state, the hills close to the river are covered with dense undergrowth and a thick forest, except for areas that have been cleared for farms or ranches .

289. Cf. the county maps in The Texas Almanac 2006-2007, Elizabeth Cruce Alvarez, Editor (Dallas: Dallas Morning News, 2006), pp. 167-326.

290. Talon, Pierre and Jean-Baptiste, "Voyage to the Mississippi,"LaSalle, the Mississippi, and the Gulf, ed. by Robert S. Weddle, translated by Ann Linda Bell, (College Station:Texas A&M University Press, 1987), p. 253.

291. "*Una India*" is translated by Flint as "an Indian woman" while Winship rendered it "an Indian girl." Pedro de Castañeda, "Narrative," in Documents of the Coronado Expedition, 1539-1542, transcribed and translated by Richard and Shirley Curshing Flint (Albuquerque: University of New Mexico Press, 2005), pp. 409, 465; The Journey of Coronado 1540-1542, translated and edited by George Parker Winship (Golden, Colorado: Fulcrum Publishing Co., 1990), p. 133. All of this will be more fully explained in a later chapter.

Chapter 9

292. Assuming there was no cloud cover.

293. Krieger, pp. 212-213 and pp. 277-278.

294. The claim that on his voyage along the Gulf Coast in 1519 Alonso Alvarez de Piñeda (d. 1520) first saw this river has been soundly repudiated. Cf. Donald E. Chipman, *Alonso Alvarez de Piñeda and the Río de las Palmas: Scholars and the Mislocation of a River*, in The Southwestern Historical Quarterly, Vol. 98, No.3 (Jan., 1995), pp. 369-385; Robert S. Weddle, *Alvarez de Pineda, Alonso*, in The Handbook of Texas Online, www.tshaonline.org/handbook/online/articles/fal 72

295. Adorno &Pautz, pp. 212, 214.

296.Adorno &Pautz, pp. 212-213. It was perhaps at 5:30 or 6:00 PM CST U. S. when they first arrived at the greatriver.

297. Adorno & Pautz, pp. 212-213.

298. Adorno &Pautz, pp. 212-213.

299.Cabeza de Vaca spelled it slightly differently: *"Traian calabacas horadadas con piedras dentro."*Adorno & Pautz, p. 194.

300. Adorno & Pautz, p. 213.

301.Adorno &Pautz, p. 213.

302. De León, Alonso, "Historia de Nuevo Leon," published and edited by Genearo Garcia in Documentos Ineditos o Muy Raros Para La Historia de Mexico, (Mexico: Editorial Porrua, S. A., 1975-reprint of the 1909 edition), p. 18. This was a history (from the late 1500s to about 1639) of the greater Cerralvo part of New Spain that was bounded roughly by the Río El Alamo, the Rio Grande, the Río San Juan, the Río Pesqueria, and the line of mountains known as the Sierra Los Picachos and the Sierra Papagayos. DeLeón the elder must not be confused with his son of the same name who was governor of Nuevo Leon and made excursions into South Texas in the 1680s.

303. Robles, Alessio, Coahuila y Texas en la Epoca Colonial, (Mexico, D. F.: Editorial Cultura, 1938), pp. 58-59 where Robles in turn follows Herbert Bolton

in <u>The Spanish Borderlands</u> (New Haven: Yale University Press, 1921), pp. 26-46.

304.De León; this is my translation of part of the last paragraph of chapter iv, p. 18.

305. Por el parte del norte,De León, p. 18.

306. Since there would not likely have been an indigenous trail that was up in the rugged mountain slopes of the Sierra Los Picachos to the west of the town of Ceralvo, which was originally built at this site to be close to the mine shafts in the mountains, the southbound path that the four took ran a short distance to the east or between Cerralvo and the town of Melchor Ocampo. The road left behind the basin of the Río El Alamo and went over the divide to meet another mountain creek (a tributary of the Río El Rancho which runs east through Melchor Ocampo into the Río San Juan and on toward Rio Grande City). A good map to assist with this pass through Cerralvo is <u>Map of Reynosa and Northeast Mexico,</u> (Corpus Christi: TexMaps, 2007; website at <u>www.TexMaps.com</u>).

307. In 1522, Cortéz began to build ships at Zacatula a short distance north of Acapulco. David J. Weber, <u>The Spanish Frontier in North America,</u> (New Haven: Yale University Press, 2009), p. 33.

308. Krieger, p. 215 and p. 280.

309. Krieger, p. 215 and p. 280.

310. Alessio Robles, Vito, <u>Monterrey en la Historia y en la Leyenda,</u>(Mexico City: Antigua Libreria Robredo, 1936), pp. 64-66.

311. Robles, p. 64-66.

312. Krieger, p. 215 and p. 280.

313. Krieger, p. 215.

314. Krieger, p. 214.
315. Krieger, p. 215, pp. 279-280.

316. Krieger, p. 280.

317. Krieger, p. 215 and pp. 279-280

318. Krieger, p. 214.

319. Wikipedia the Free Encyclopedia, s.v."
"http://en.wikipedia.org/wiki/Luis_de_Carabajal_y _Cueva" (accessed May 22, 2010), and "http://en.wikipedia.org/wiki/Alberto_del_Canto" (accessed May 22, 2010).

320. *Cerralvo*, Enciclopedia de los Municipios de Mexico, s.v. http://www.inafed.gob.mx/ work/templates/enciclo/nuevoleon/municipios/19001a.htm.

321. In *Historia General,* Oviedo, so it appears, simply skipped over the spans in the *Joint Report* that applied to the first 42.5 miles on the Cerralvo Trail; he did include the last few distances that totaled 37.5 miles down toPlatita. Krieger, pp. 278-279.

322. Krieger,pp. 214-215.

323. Krieger, p. 213.

324 Krieger, p. 214.

325. Krieger, p. 214.

326.Krieger, p. 213-215 and pp. 278-279; it appears that in this village the grisly identifying mark was to punch out one eye of every one in the band.

327. Krieger, p. 215;cf. Map of Reynosa and Northeast Mexico, (Corpus Christi: TexMaps, 2007 www.texmaps.com). In the heights of the Sierra de los Picachos, it rained a lot more than in the surrounding country.

328. Krieger, p. 279 and p. 214. They passed near the site of the town of General Treviño.

329.Krieger, p. 214.

330.Krieger, p. 215; cf. Joaquín Palacios Roji García, Guia Roji Por Las Carreteras de Mexico, (Mexico City: Guia Roji, S. A. de C. V., 1997), p. 21-22. The Sierra Madre, whose highest mountains rise to over 8,000 feet, did not, as they thought, "come unbroken from" the Gulf of Mexico, for the Sierra de San Carlos is a separate mountain range between the escarpment of the Sierra Madre and the seashore.

331. Goodwin, Robert,Crossing the Continent, (London: Harper Collins

Publishers, 2008), p. 21; Goodwin makes the case that Esteban was a black African who, to escape famine, actually may have desired to be sold into slavery.

332. Goodwin says that Esteban was the "savior" of the other three on the journey.

333. Krieger, p. 279.

334. Robles, Alessio, <u>Coahuila y Texas en la Epoca Colonial</u> (Mexico, D. F.: Editorial Cultura, 1938), pp. 58- 59.

335. Krieger, pp. 215-216.

Chapter 10

336. Krieger, p. 222.

337. When Cabeza de Vaca wrote that they passed through on the plain between the two ranges and "near" the mountains (*cerca de las sierras*) that came up from the coast or the Sierra Madre Oriental, he made a minor mistake; the river and the terrain tell us that in fact they passed "near" the other mountains, the much smaller Papagayos. Adorno & Pauck, Vol. I, pp. 200-201; Krieger, pp. 215-216 and p. 280.

338. Krieger, p. 215 and pp. 279-280.

339. Krieger, p. 224. From Platita the four followed a succession of old roads that merchants may have used, in the late 1400s and the earlier 1500s, to go to Tenochtitlán (later Mexico City) and the Aztec Empire far to the south where they offered in trade such goods as silver nuggets, buffalo hides, and pine nuts. Still earlier, in the 1200s and 1300s, carriers and traders of the scarlet macaw may have used the path, coming up from the rainforests of southern Tamaulipas, where the birds thrived at that time, to arrive at Mimbres in central New Mexico and Paquimé (Casas Grandes) in northwest Chihuahua where remains of the colorful birds have been found. Cf. Darrell Creel and Charmion McKusick, *Prehistoric Macaws and Parrots in the Mimbres Area, New Mexico,* (Journal of American Antiquity, Vol. 59, No. 3, Jul., 1994, pp. 510),accessed online August 21, 2019, <u>www.jstor.org/stable/282463?seq=#page_scan_tab_contents</u>.

340. Krieger, p. 220.

341. Krieger, p. 224.

342. Krieger, p. 224. Although here and there he made a few mistakes, on this matter Cabeza de Vaca knew exactly what he was writing; he was describing their journey as one across the continent from east coast to west.

343.Krieger, p. 283. I found no corroboration of the wide use of a second oral language. In other words, they were not using a *langua franca*, just the signs.

344. Krieger, p. 213.

345.Krieger, p.217-218 and pp. 280-282.

346. Krieger, p. 281.

347. Krieger, p. 281. Oviedo copied the phrase "straight to the north," but he put it in the wrong place.

348. Adorno &Pautz, pp. 204-205 and Krieger, p. 281.The four made three one-day trips as part of a journey of some eighty leagues (240 miles), including a travel segment "by the skirts of the mountains."

349. Krieger, p. 217 & p. 281. In an attempt to aptly describe the spectacular vistas of these steep mountain slopes, Cabeza de Vaca used the archaic Spanish word *haldas,* which later became *faldas* and means either skirts or slopes. I discussed this briefly with Professor Sonia Cania of the University of Texas at Arlington.

350. Both creeks can be seen easily using Google Earth.

351. Krieger, p. 217 and p. 281.

352. Krieger, p. 217. They had made another one-day trek of about thirty miles, indicated by their arrival at night.

353. Donald W. Olson, et al, Piñon Pines and the Route of Cabeza de Vaca, reprinted at the website of the Texas State Historical Association http://www.tsha.utexas.edu from the October 1997 issue of the Southwestern Historical Quarterly. (AccessedaboutOctober 1, 2008).

354. Cf. *Altos Hornos de Mexico*, in Wikipedia [no author listed] <http://en.wikipedia.org/wiki/ Altos_Hornos_de_Mexico>, accessed March 23, 2010. In 1942, a company was formed and based in Monclova to make steel from the metal deposits taken from mines in the region, although by the early 2000s, better iron ore was brought in by train from other parts of Coahuila. Because of its large factory that, from the iron, produced steel, used for instance

198

in the manufacture of automobiles, Monclova gained the reputation as *la capital de acero de Mexico*, the steel capital of Mexico.

355.Krieger, p. 217. The Río Monclova flows into the Río Salado de Nadadores whose waters empty into the Rio Grande at Falcon Reservoir; the Río El Salado is not the same as the Río Salado; the Sabinas of Nuevo Leon (not to be confused with the Sabinas of Coahuila) turns back east and also empties into Falcon Reservoir and the Rio Grande .

356. Krieger, p. 217.

357. In a later chapter, there will be more about the bison in Mexico; cf. List, Rurik, Ceballos, Gerardo, et al, "Historic Distribution and Challenges to Bison Recovery in the Northern Chihuahuan Desert," Journal of Conservation Biology, (Boston: Dec. 2007, Vol. 21, No. 6), pp. 1487-1494.

358. Krieger, p. 282. From Platita (near Los Ramones) the distance to Cascabel, according to the two narratives, was approximately 250 miles, and from Los Rios Tres on the Nueces River, "where they began to walk," it was estimated to have been about 450 miles.

359. Krieger, p. 282.

360. Michael E. Smith, The Aztecs, Second Edition, (Malden, MA: Blaackwell Publishing, 2003), pp. 269-271; also cf. Raul Ybarra, Anatomy of Prehispanic Bells, https://exarc.net/ark/88735/10044. Accessed September 8, 2019

361. They will eventually mount a long trail that was, in part, the same as the *Camino Real de La Tierra Adentro,* the Royal Road of the Interior that later linked Santa Fe to Mexico City. Jacques Soustelle, Daily Life of the Aztecs (London: Phoenix Press, 2003, originally published in France in 1955), pp. 26, 59, 232.

362. Krieger, pp. 217-218, 281.

363. Adorno &Pautz, Vol I, pp 208-209.

364. Krieger, p. 281.

365. Krieger, pp. 217-218.

366. Krieger, pp. 217-218.

367. Krieger, pp. 217-218. Most of the books speculate that the nation of

cascabels to the north was a reference to the indigenous people of New Mexico. However, while the Pueblo people who lived there were farmers and had permanent adobe houses, some with three or four levels, they did not possess the skill of smelting copper and other metals to make decorative objects. The place of origin of the copper *cascabel* was the Aztec city of Tenochtitlán or one of the other cities in the Valley of Mexico.

Chapter 11

368. Krieger, pp. 234-235.

369. Krieger, p. 218.

370. Mike Cox, Cabeza de Vaca, M. D., www.texasescapes.com/MikeCoxTexasTales/Cabeza-de-Vaca-MD.htm,.

371. Mike Cox.

372.Krieger, pp. 218-219.

373.Krieger, pp. 218-219.

374. Few, if any, of his numerous alterations in the second draft, (that of Valladolid in 1555) touched important geographic issues so as to clarify the first edition (that of Zamora in 1542). For more about the two editions, see Adorno & Pautz, Vol. I, pp. xv-xxiv.

375. Krieger, p. 282.

376."*Por aquellos valles,*" Adorno & Pautz, p. 210 of Vol. L. Although there was abundant water with native villages to the northwest (along the Río Santa Elena) and also to the northeast (toward Nueva Rosita and the Río Sabinas), on the La Boquilla Trail, they turned west to go along the upstream path of the Río Nadadores.

377. Based on information on Google Earth. This site corresponds with the hint in the narrative that it came relatively soon after the departure from Río Hermoso (south of Castaños). The rabbits prefer, during the day, to hide in areas of dense undergrowth. Although Cabeza de Vaca does not name a particular flora, the rabbits would have surely fled when a group of men approached, unless they were hiding in some form of vegetative cover.

378. Based on Google Earth and on information provided by Javier Garcia

200

Govea, Accessed on February 26, 2009. Mr. Garcia Govea informs that the southernmost part is called the *Valle de Las Calaveras* while farther to the north, it is called the *Valle de Hundido*. In August and September,Coahuila receives more rain than falls the rest of the year.

379. From here the La Boquilla Trail probably ran near the later site of La Presita, now following to the north and downstream a tributary of the Río La Boquilla a few miles east of San Guillermo, near the area of the small Mexican pueblos of San Miguel and Piedritas. Cf. Roji Garcia, Joaquin Palacios, y Roji Garcia, Agustin Palacios, Guia Roji Por Las Carreteras de Mexico, (Ciudad de Mexico: GuiaRoji, S. A. de C. V. 1997), pp. 19-20.

380. Krieger, p. 219. Several route scholars have mistakenly followed Krieger.

381. Krieger, pp. 76-78.

Chapter 12

382. Krieger, pp. 225-226. The quote is amplified and paraphrased.

383. Krieger, pp. 231-232.

384. There is nothing in the narratives to suggest that they arrived at the Rio Grande and drank its water but did not cross it, or that they made a difficult trek from the head of the Rio Babia-Alamos across part of the Chihuahuan Desert without enough water to drink, prior to this crossing, which would have been a notable event on the way and therefore, worthy of some mention in the narrative.

385. Krieger, pp. 218-219, and p. 282.

386. Cf. Paul Horgan, Great River: The Rio Grande in North American History, (Hanover, NH: Wesleyan University Press, 1984), p. 851; Jay W. Sharp, "Desert Trails: Major Native American Trails," http://www.desertusa. com/mag03/trails/trails02.html, (11/24/2006).

387. From the blog of "The Texas Bohemian" (no name published), "The Power of Big Bend," http://www.associatedcontent.com/article/54239/the_power_of_big_bend_pg 4.html?cat=16 (accessed 3/2/2011). The Comanches did not enter the Big Bend region until much later.

388.The outline of the Marathon Basin runs roughly from just southwest of the town northeast along Highway 385 and can be seen on Google Earth; cf. the map of Brewster County in <u>Texas Almanac 2010-2011</u>, edited by Elizabeth Cruce Alvarez (Denton: Texas State Historical Association, 2010), p. 227.

389. "… Y passados unos llanos de treinta leguas hallamos mucha gente que de lexos de allí venia a rescebirnos." Adorno & Pautz, p. 212

390. Cf. Robert Goodwin, <u>Crossing the Continent 1527-1540,</u> (London: Harper, 2008), pp. 150-151, 186. Goodwin doubts that Cabeza de Vaca is trying to give an honest account.

391. Early F. McBride, Geology of the Marathon Uplift (Geological Society of America Centennial Field Guide, South-Central Section, 1988, <u>http://rockfractureandstress.com/</u>.)

392. Krieger, pp. 218-219.

393.They departed Tiguex, (on the Rio Grande near Bernalillo, New Mexico, a few miles north of Albuquerque). This is based on records and letters of Pedro de Castañeda y Najera, Juan Jaramillo and other members of the Coronado expedition; George Parker Winship, editor, <u>The Journey of Coronado: 1540-1542</u>, translated and edited by George Parker Winship, (Golden, Colorado: Fulcrum Publishing, 1990), p. 132.

394.<u>Cf</u>. Turner, Dorothy (Librarian), "Coronado Expedition Artifacts" at website of Floyd County Museum, <u>http://www.floydcountymuseum.com</u>.

395. Winship, p. 208.

396.Winship, p. 208.

397. Krieger, p. 282.

398. Winship, p. 132. The gifts were of such things as bags of pine nuts or arrowheads.

399. Diego Perez de Luxán, "Account," in <u>Rediscovery of New Mexico Vol. III</u>, translated and edited by George P. Hamond and Agapito Rey, (Albuquerque: University of New Mexico Press, 1966), pp. 162-165.

400. Krieger, p. 219. Having earlier at the mouth of the Arroyo La Minita (near Ciudad Mier) made a first crossing, the four travelers, now in these "far away" regions, made a second crossing of a "*gran rio*," followed by a walk of ninety miles up to an area of some plains and then over an unknown distance to

Recepción and the four other villages; the final or third crossing, (where it came "up to the chest"), was preceded by a walk of more than 150 miles over the Candelaria Trail from Recepción back to, (not necessarily the great river itself but to), the ford on the Rio Grande. Consequently, the native village of Recepción, the first of the five villages on a stream or river, must have been somewhere near the Pecos River.

401. On the north side of the Glass Mountains, the trail probably followed the creek later called Six Shooter Draw. Then, at about the point where the state highway 385 crosses, the trail may have cut overland to the northwest to follow Comanche Creek north to the gushing Comanche Springs near Ft. Stockton.

402.Luxán, pp. 162-165.These villages could not have been on the Delaware River because it is too far from the La Junta region, and to follow its upstream path would not have led back to the south and to the Rio Grande. It could not have been a site on the Pecos River because Espejo turned away from following the Pecos; also, the trail that went through the five villages led them back, within a distance of about 150 miles, to the Rio Grande at San Bernardino in the region just north of La Junta de Los Rios, which a trail along the Pecos would not have done.

Chapter 13

403. Krieger, p. 277.

404. Krieger, p. 277.

405. Krieger, p. 277. This is my amplification and paraphrase of what I believe he was trying to say.

406. Krieger, p. 219. Again, this is my amplification and paraphrase of his words.

407. The strip of land along the banks of Toyah Creek was verdant and alive like this until, in 1871, they began to drain away the creek water for irrigation.

408.Krieger, p. 220 and p. 283.

409. Krieger, p. 220 and p. 283.

410. Krieger, p. 283.

411. Krieger, pp. 220-221. This is my paraphrase and amplification of what I

believe he was trying to say.

412. Luxán's *Account of the Espejo Expedition* in Hammond and Rey, Rediscovery of New Mexico, pp. 209-210. Luxán and Espejo provide a fuller, more-detailed description of the trail than does Cabeza de Vaca.

413. Krieger, p. 220-221.

414. Krieger p. 220 and p. 283. The path did not go through Limpia Canyon, the site of Fort Davis, then down Alamito Creek, for by it, there are neither two canyons, nor twenty-four miles of plains, nor the rugged, dry mountains, nor the pools of water, and it is much farther than 150 miles to the ford at San Bernardino.

415. Hammond and Rey, p. 229.

416. Luxán, pp. 209-210.

417. Luxán, pp. 209-210.

418. Krieger, p. 220 and p. 283.

419. "La Junta Indians," Wikipedia, https://en.wikipedia.org/wiki/La_Junta_Indians.

420. Luxán, pp. 209-210.

421. It was said to be a little more than forty leagues; Espejo made a little blunder by recording that it was the distance "to the Conchos" instead of to the Rio Grande; this is evident because the distance from Recepción near the mouth of Toyah Creek to the Conchos on the Candelaria Trail and over the Sierra El Peguís, would have been at least 170 miles, (not 123), and about the same distance by Alamito Creek to the Conchos mouth. cf. Luxán in Hammond and Rey, p. 229.

422. Krieger, p. 220 and p. 283.

423. Krieger, p. 220.

424. Hammond and Rey, p. 210. The site of San Bernardino harmonizes with the descent out of the dry mountains, the pass over some plains, and the other landmarks *only* if it were fifteen miles *upstream* and north from the confluence, as per the Espejo records, since, at that point downstream, (near the village of Redford), the rugged terrain, and the lack of a fresh-water creek (that

connected to the Davis Mountains), render an approach from the north unlikely.

425. <u>Texas Atlas & Gazetteer,</u> (Yarmouth, Maine: DeLorme, 2005), p. 51,52, and 63.

426. <u>Texas Atlas & Gazetteer,</u> (Yarmouth, Maine: DeLorme, 2005), pp. 51,52, and 63.

427. Krieger, p. 220; and p.283; perhaps the guides wanted no heavy bags to burden them as they traversed again the difficult pass up into the Sierra Vieja.

428. *"Un río muy grande que el agua nos dava hasta los pechos,"* Adorno & Pautz, p. 214; cf. Krieger, p.219 and pp. 282-283.

429. Krieger, p. 220. In 1581, Gallegos and those in the Rodríguez party took this Casas Grandes Trail, while rejecting another road "to the north," the Candelaria Trail. Travelers of that age who wished to go to Casas Grandes or to the Pacific coast, cut away to the west from the Rio Grande while those going into New Mexico continued to the north.

430. Krieger, p. 220.From Río Hermoso, following the route proposed here, the approximate distance to the ford at the southern tip of the Big Bend on the Rio Grande, was 260 miles, which they could have made in twelve to twenty days. From the Rio Grande crossing to the village of Recepción on Toyah Creek near the Pecos River, was another 200 miles or so which they could have made in ten to fifteen more days. From here along the 150-mile Candelaria Trail they could have arrived at San Bernardino (north by northwest of Presidio) after a journey of twelve to twenty more days.

Chapter 14

431. In 1619, a group of African slaves disembarked in Virginia. Esteban had arrived in Florida over 90 years earlier.

432. Krieger, p. 285-286.

433. The Casas Grandes Trail also has been referred to as the "Shell Trail." If it followed the only fresh water available, the path may have meandered between the intermittent river mouths and dry lakes: the Río del Carmen on the Laguna de Patos, (near Villa Ahumada), the Río Santa Maria on the Laguna de Santa Maria, and the Río Casas Grandes on the Laguna de Guzmán.

434. Krieger, p. 221.

435.This is based on hints in the narrative plus the reality on the ground and from what other native people later told those of the Sanchez-Rodriguez and Espejo expeditions.

436. Cf. Krieger, pp. 76-78. We can see that as to this part of the journey, the major alternative proposal that broadly follows Davenport, is mistaken, along with all the variations thereof. The four did not go through the region of Nueva Rosita and up the Río Babia and the Río Alamos (i.e. the tributaries of the Río Sabinas of Coahuila and the Río Salado). Nor did they try to cross the Chihuahua Desert without going to the Rio Grande at the southern tip of the Big Bend.

437. Krieger, p. 221. This is a paraphrase and amplification of what I believe he was trying to say.

438. *"Diximos que queriamos ir a la puesta del sol,"* Cabeza de Vaca, Alvar Nunez, "The 1542 Relacion," translated byRolena Adorno and Patrick Charles Pautz, in <u>Álvar Nuñez Cabeza de Vaca, Vol. I,</u> (Lincoln: University of Nebraska Press, 1999), p. 214.

439.The first expedition was under the charge of Francisco Sánchez Chamuscado (1521?-1582), *Cf.* Diego Perez de Luxán, *The Account* (of the Espejo Expedition of 1582-83), and Antonio Espejo, "Report," both in G. Hammond and R. Rey, <u>Rediscovery of New Mexico 1580-1594,</u> (Alberquerque: University of New Mexico Press, 1966), p.160 and pp. 216-217

440. Hernán Gallegos, "Relation," in <u>Rediscovery of New Mexico Vol. III,</u> translated and edited by George P. Hamond and Agapito Rey (Albuquerque: University of New Mexico Press, 1966), pp. 75 and 71-73.

441. The Antonio Espejo group apparently set up camp somewhere near the eastern base of the mountains, and the next day, they followed the Jumano guides due east about nine miles to the San Bernadino on the Rio Grande. Ibid, Espejo, p. 217.

442.Krieger,p. 75 and pp. 71-73.

443. Thanks to Patricia Sims of the Presidio High School who shared this local information with me.

444. Krieger, p. 222.

445. Krieger, p. 222.

446. The Rodríguez missionary expedition of 1581-82 was a direct response to *Los Naufragios* by Cabeza de Vaca, who stated that the native people would readily convert, if given compassionate treatment.

447. The route taken in 1535 to the southern tip of the Big Bend fits remarkably well with the conditions on the ground and with what we would expect to have been the footpath taken by earlier explorers from Tamaulipus to Casas Grandes and other sites to the northwest along this La Boquilla Trail. In the 1850s the Americans discovered various branches of the Commanche Trail and other native roads that had been used for centuries.

448. Krieger, p. 284.

449.Krieger, p. 284.

450. Krieger, pp. 172-173. This is my paraphrase and amplification.

451. The two women were separated from the main group by five days. The Spaniards spent fifteen days with the people of San Bernardino: one or two days at the village itself, five or six one-day trips to Enojados followed by three days of waiting, three days of travel beyond, and two days waiting for Castillo and Esteban to do a reconnaissance. It took at least one full day from San Bernardino to cross over to the west side of the mountains; the four Spaniards then trekked seventy to eighty miles to Enojados, the waiting place in five or six one-day trips.

452. Krieger, pp. 220-222 and pp. 284-286.

453. Oviedo attempted to interpret his copy of the *Joint Report* to unite as one the recorded descriptions of two different events, a mistake that he made at several places; he combined the dialogue with the San Bernardino people at Enojados with another exchange with the Jumanos some days later at the village here called Vacas Sur.Krieger, p. 285.

454. Of the various erroneous interpretations of this incident none is more bizarre than the theory that the four split up to travel long distances apart from one another and only later rejoined to go up the Rio Grande to El Paso. cf. Robert Goodwin, <u>Crossing the Continent 1527-1540</u>, (London: Harper, 2008), pp. 278-282.

455.Antonio Espejo, "Report," in Hamond and Rey, pp. 216-217.

456. Hammond and Rey, pp. 216-217.

457. Hammond and Rey, p. 160.

458.Hammond and Rey, p. 160 and pp. 216-217.

459. Hammond and Rey, p. 164; Cabeza de Vaca did not go to the mouth of the Conchos; the people from that area may have gone to see him at San Bernardino which was, from La Junta, less than a one-day, fifteen-mile walk.

460. Hammond and R. Rey, p. 164. From San Bernardino to Enojados and then to Vacas Norte was equal to seven to nine one-day trips (about 150 miles). Between 1535 and 1582, the Jumanos, to find more riparian lands to grow corn, squash, and beans, migrated north, yet they still lived along the Río Conchos. East and west of the Conchos at the Presa de La Rosetilla, the mountains on both sides rise to an elevation of over 4,000 feet. I found them using Google Earth.

461. Hammond and Rey, pp.160-161. Cabeza de Vaca and his group manifestly did not cross the Chihuahuan Desert between CuatroCiénegas and Jiménez, where there was not enough water, to arrive somewhere on the Río Florido and then to travel north downstream the Conchos, a proposition that would leave unexplained solid pieces of evidence for the travel of the four deep into the Trans-Pecos, Texas region.

462. Hammond and Rey, pp.160-161

463. Krieger, p. 226. About the year A.D. 1410, Native Americans with clay pots, farming skills, and permanent houses, abandoned the region, after living on the banks of the Rio Grande and the Conchos near its mouth. Yet, by A.D. 1581, the Jumanos and others had moved into the area and possessed all three things.

464. These observations are based on the archaeological findings of J. Charles Kelley and others as summarized by A. Cloud and A. Krieger. Cf. Andy Cloud, "La Junta's Remarkable Past," at the La Junta Heritage Center website, www.lajuntaheritage.org; cf. Alex Krieger, We Came Naked and Barefoot, (Austin: University of Texas Press, 2002), pp. 93-94.

465. Cerca de alli y por aquel rio arriba mas de cincuenta leguas. Adorno & Pautz, Vol. I, p. 222.

466. List, Rurik, Ceballos, Gerardo, et al, "Historic Distribution and Challenges to Bison Recovery in the Northern Chihuahuan Desert," Journal of

Conservation Biology, (Boston: December 2007, Vol. 21, No. 6), pp. 1487-1494.

467. Among several reports of sightings in northern Mexico, in 1806, a zoologist saw herds in the region near Monterrey, Nuevo Leon. Tom McHugh, The Time of the Buffalo, (Edison, NJ: Castle Books, 2004), p. 174.

468. Lew Wallace, "A Buffalo Hunt in Northern Mexico," in Mexican Game Trails: Americans Afield in Old Mexico, 1866-1940, edited by Neil Carmony and David Brown (Norman: University ofOklahoma Press, 1991), pp. 11-29.

Chapter 15

469. Krieger, p. 222.

470. Krieger, p. 286.

471. Krieger, pp. 222-224 and pp. 286-287.

472. Krieger, p. 287. To join the hunt with "all" the others of their village who were already there, Oviedo recorded in *Historia General*, many of these people would soon walk "to the north" where the bison graze and which was a distance of a three-day walk or fifty to sixty miles; Oviedo, who frequently combines disparate material, has mistakenly linked this reference with some unrelated lines that must have been a little farther down in the *Joint Report*. The statement about the desire to soon travel to the bison herds harmonizes with a three-day trip from there at Vacas Sur near La Boquilla to the grassy plains along the Río Florido or the Río Parral.

473. Krieger, pp. 223.

474.Krieger, p. 285. Oviedo inadvertently helps here by adding in *Historia General*, although out of proper context, as usual, that the trail to "the cows .... was up toward the north," and along it, they would find "people" or villages along the way in distinction from the other one, the Ataros Trail, up the Río Conchos that was "toward the west" from Vacas Sur.

475.Krieger, p. 286.

476. Krieger, p. 224.

477. Krieger, p. 286.

478. Krieger, p.224 and p. 286.

479. Caminamos ... a la puesta del sol por unos llanos y entre unas sierras muy grandes..., Adorno and Pautz, Vol. 1, p. 228.

480. Based on information and images in the appropriate parts of Google Earth.

481. Krieger's translation of this line is questionable: "...at sunset [traveling] through some plains and between some very large mountains which arise there, we found there a people ...," Krieger, p. 224.

482.Krieger, p.224.

483.Krieger, p. 287.

484. The narratives suggest that they arrived at Corazones in mid or late December 1535; Krieger, p.227and p. 289.

485. Krieger, p.224 and p. 287.

486. Krieger, p. 286.The two reservoirs are the Presa Plutarco Elias Calles and the Presa Alvaro Obregón.

487. Cabeza de Vaca, "Los Naufragios," Vol. I, Adorno and Pautz, p. 234.

488. Thanks to my brother Kenard P. Sharp for giving me information about his hunting trip to the region in the 1990s.

489. Krieger, p.227 and 229.

490. Obregón, Baltasar de, Chronicles of the Discoveries of New Spain, (1584).

491. Obregón, pp. 201-220.

492. Vanderwood, Paul J., The Power of God Against the Guns of Government (Loma Linda: Stanford University Press, 1998), p. 103.

493.Obregón, p. 202.

494.Obregón, p. 202.

495.The young man, motivated by his encounter with Ibarra, may have arrived at his Jumano home in the Valle de Zaragoza after only five to six days, breathless with his exciting news that such men were camped near Yepomera, which would make the total turnaround some fifteen to twenty-one days. Obregón, p. 202.

496. Krieger, p. 225.

497. Krieger, p. 289.

498. Krieger p. 289 and p. 218.

499. Cf. Michael Smith, <u>The Aztecs</u>, p. 96.

500. By 1555, after years of lawsuits and appeals, Cabeza de Vaca was "currying favor with the Spanish crown … unmistakably" demonstrating that he was "a royal intimate again." Morrow, Baker H., <u>The South American Expeditions, 1540-1545</u> (Albuquerque: University of New Mexico Press: 2011), p. 195; He died sometime after 1560. Resendez, Andres, <u>A Land so Strange</u>, (New York: Basic Books: 2007), pp. 221.

Bibliography

I.   About the Journey

Adorno, Rolena and Patrick C. Pautz. <u>Álvar Núñez Cabeza de Vaca</u>, Vol.1-3. Lincoln: University of NebraskaPress, 1999.

Bishop, Morris. <u>The Odyssey of Cabeza de Vaca</u>. New York: The Century Company, 1933.
Chipman, Donald E. <u>ÁlvarNúñez Cabeza de Vaca: The Great Pedestrian</u>. Denton: Texas State Historical Association,2012.

Davenport, Harbert, and James B. Wells. 1918 and 1919. "The First Europeans in Texas, 1528-1536." <u>Southwestern Historical Quarterly</u> 22(2): 111-142 and 22(3): 205-259, accessed January 28, 2009,<u>http://www.tshaonline.org/shqonline/apager.php?vol.022</u>.

Goodwin, Robert, <u>Crossing the Continent.</u> London: Harper Collins Publishers, 2008.

Krieger, Alex. <u>We Came Naked and Barefoot.</u> Austin: University of Texas Press, 1999.

Reséndez, Andrés. <u>A Land So Strange</u>. New York: Basic Books, 2007.

Schneider, Paul. <u>Brutal Journey</u>. New York: Henry Holt & Co., LLC, 2006.

Varnum, Robin. <u>Álvar Núñez Cabeza de Vaca: American Trailblazer</u>. Norman: University of Oklahoma Press, 2014.

212

II. Primary Sources in Original Spanish

Adorno, Rolena and Patrick C. Pautz. <u>Álvar Núñez Cabeza de Vaca</u>, Vol.1-3. Lincoln: University of Nebraska Press, 1999.

De León, Alonso, "Historia de Nuevo Leon," published and edited by Genearo Garcia in <u>Documentos Ineditos o Muy Raros Para La Historia de Mexico</u>, (Mexico: Editorial Porrua, S. A., 1975-reprint of the 1909 edition), p. 18.

Oviedo y Valdes, Gonzalo Fernandez de, "The Account of the Narvaez Expedition." Transcribed and translated by Basil C. Hedrick and Carroll L. Riley, in <u>The Journey of the Vaca Party</u>. Carbondale: Southern Illinois University Press, 1974.

III. Other Articles, Websites and Books Consulted

"Exhibits" by Dorothy Turner. Librarian at the Floyd County Museum website, floydcountymuseum.com.

"Mitchell Ridge." Texas Beyond History website, accessed May 20, 2010, http://www.texasbeyondhistory.net/mitchell/investigations.html.

"San Antonio de Valero Mission." <u>Handbook of Texas Online</u>, s.v., accessed August 6, 2009,http://www.tshaonline.org/ handbook/online/articles/SS/uqs8.html.

Alessio Robles, Vito. <u>Monterrey en la Historia y en la Leyenda.</u> Mexico City: Antigua Libreria Robredo, 1936.

Bedichek, Roy. <u>Adventures with a Texas Naturalist.</u> Austin: University of Texas Press, 1947. pp.139-140.

Cartwright, Gary. <u>Galveston A History</u>. Fort Worth: TCU Press,1991.

Castañeda, Pedro de. "Narrative." <u>Documents of the Coronado Expedition, 1539-1542.</u>Transcribed and translated by Flint, Richard and Shirley Curshing Flint. Albuquerque: University of New MexicoPress, 2005.

Cerralvo, Enciclopedia de los Municipios de Mexico, s.v., accessed May 22, 2010, http://www.inafed.gob.mx/ work/templates/enciclo/nuevoleon/municipios/19001a.htm.

Chipman, Donald E. "Malhado Island." The Handbook of Texas Online,accessed June 2, 2008,http://www.tshaonline.org/handbook/online/articles/MM/rrm1.html.

Chipman, Donald E. *Alonso Alvarez de Piñeda and the Río de las Palmas: Scholars and the Mislocation of a River.* The Southwestern Historical Quarterly. Vol. 98, No.3, January, 1995. pp. 369-385

Chipman, Donald E. Spanish Texas: 1519-1821, Austin: University of Texas Press, 1992.

Clay, Comer, and Diana J. Kleiner. "Colorado River." The Handbook of Texas Online, accessed August 18, 2009,http://www.tshaonline.org/handbook/online/articles/CC/rnc10.html.

Cloud, Andy, "La Junta's Remarkable Past." La Junta Heritage Center website, accessed March 9, 2010.www.lajuntaheritage.org

Davis, William C. The Pirate Lafitte. New York: Harcourt Inc. 2005

Foster, William C. Texas & Northeastern Mexico: 1630-1690. Austin: University of Texas Press, 1997

Griffin, S. C. History of Galveston, Texas. Galveston: A. H. Cawston, 1931.

Hall, Grant D. and Black, Steven, et al. "Archeological Investigations at Choke Canyon Reservoir..." and "Hunter-Gatherer Life along the Frio River in the South Texas Brush Country."Texas Beyond History website, accessed October 14, 2008, www.texasbeyondhistory.net/choke/.

Hammond, G. and A. Rey, Rediscovery of New Mexico 1580-1594 (Albuquerque: University of New Mexico Press, 1966)

Hendricks, Frances, et al, ed.San Antonio in the Eighteenth Century. San Antonio: Bicentennial Heritage Committee, 1976.

Horgan, Paul. Great River: The Rio Grande in North American History. Hanover, NH: Wesleyan University Press, 1984. p. 851.

Huddleston, Scott."Historic Items Found near San Antonio River." Dallas Morning News. Sunday, November 7, 2010, originally published in the San Antonio Express-News, p. 5A

Jordan, Terry G., et al.Texas: A Geography. Boulder, Colorado: Westview

214

Press, 1984.

Las Casas, Bartolomé de. <u>A Short Account of the Destruction of the Indies</u>, [original version published 1542].Translated by Nigel Griffin. London: Penguin Books, 1992.

List, Rurik, Ceballos, Gerardo, et al. "Historic Distribution and Challenges to Bison Recovery in the Northern Chihuahuan Desert." <u>Journal of Conservation Biology.</u> Boston: December 2007, Vol. 21, No. 6. pp. 1487-1494

<u>Map of Reynosa and Northeast Mexico</u>. Corpus Christi: TexMaps, 2007.<u>www.TexMaps.com</u>.

McBride, Early F. Geology of the Marathon Uplift. Geological Society of America Centennial Field Guide, South-Central Section, 1988.<u>http://rockfractureandstress.com/</u>.

Morton, Robert A. "Historical Changes in the … Barrier Islands." <u>Open File Report 2007-116 U. S. Geological Survey</u>. St. Petersburg, Florida: U. S. Department of the Interior, 2007, accessed February 26, 2008,www.pubs.usgs.gov./of/2007

Obregón, Baltasar de. Chronicles of the Discoveries of New Spain.1584.

Oliver, Alice W., "Notes on the Carancahua Indians," edited by Albert S. Gatschet.<u>The Karankawa Indians, the Coast People of Texas</u>. Cambridge, Mass.: Peabody Museum, 1891.

Olson, Donald W., et al. <u>Piñon Pines and the Route of Cabeza de Vaca</u>. Reprinted at the website of the Texas State Historical Association, accessed October 1, 2008, <u>http://www.tsha.utexas.edu</u> from the October 1997 issue of the Southwestern Historical Quarterly.

Perez de Luxán, Diego. "The Account" (of the Espejo expedition of 1582-83).Edited by G. Hammond and A. Rey, <u>Rediscovery of New Mexico 1580-1594</u>. Albuquerque: University of New Mexico Press, 1966.

Pratt, Willis W., ed. Galveston Island, Or, A Few Months off the Coast of Texas 1839-40, The Journal of Francis C. Sheridan. Austin, University of Texas Press, 1954.

Ricklis, Robert A., "Cabeza de Vaca's Observations …" At the website of the Center for the Study of the Southwest, accessed May 30, 2010,<u>http://swrhc.txstate.edu/cssw/resources/cdvwindows/ricklis.ph</u>

Roads of Texas, The. Addison, TX: Mapsco Inc., 2008

Robles, Alessio. Coahuila y Texas en la Epoca Colonial. Mexico, D. F.: Editorial Cultura, 1938.\\

RojiGarcia, Joaquin Palacios, Guia Roji Por Las Carreteras de Mexico. Ciudad de Mexico: Guia Roji, S. A. de C. V, 1997.

Saxon, Lyle. Lafitte the Pirate. Gretna: Pelican Publishing Company, 1999.

Sharp, Jay W. "Desert Trails: Major Native American Trails." http://www.desertusa. com/mag03/trails/trails02.html.November 24, 2006

Smith, Michael E. The Aztecs, Second Edition. Malden, MA: Blackwell Publishing, 2003. pp. 269-271.

Soustelle, Jacques. Daily Life of the Aztecs. London: Phoenix Press, 2003.Originally published in France in 1955. pp. 26, 59, and 232

Texas Almanac 2006-2007, edited by Elizabeth Cruce Alvarez. Dallas: Dallas Morning News, 2006

Texas Atlas & Gazetteer. Yarmouth, Maine: DeLorme, 2005

Texas Tech University Center for Geospatial Technology website, accessed at various times in 2007-2009, including September 23, 2009, http://www.gis.ttu.edu/center/.
Vanderwood, Paul J., The Power of God Against the Guns of Government. Loma Linda: Stanford University Press, 1998.

Wallace, Lew. "A Buffalo Hunt in Northern Mexico," in Mexican Game Trails: AmericansAfield in Old

Webber, Robert S., La Salle, the Mississippi, and the Gulf. College Station: Texas A&M University Press, 1987,

Weddle, Robert S. San Juan Bautista Gateway to Spanish Texas. Austin: University of Texas Press, 19Weddle, Robert S. Spanish Sea: The Gulf of Mexico in North American Discovery,1500-1685. College Station: Texas A&M University Press, 1985.

Winship, George Parker. translated and edited by The Journey of Coronado 1540-1542.Golden, Colorado: Fulcrum Publishing Co., 1990.

Made in the USA
Coppell, TX
06 April 2021